D1202183

Tiger Woods

Titles in the People in the News series include:

PEOPLE
IN THE NEWS

Tiger Woods

by Michael V. Uschan

Lucent Books, San Diego, CA

Library of Congress Cataloging-in-Publication Data

Uschan, Michael V., 1948–
  Tiger Woods / by Michael V. Uschan.
    p. cm. — (People in the news)
  Includes bibliographical references (p.   ) and index.
  Summary: Discusses the life and career of Tiger Woods, including his childhood, early fame, success as the greatest amateur golfer ever, and achievements as a professional player.
  ISBN 1-56006-528-1 (alk. paper)
  1. Woods, Tiger—Juvenile literature. 2. Golfers—United States—Biography—Juvenile literature. [1. Woods, Tiger. 2. Golfers. 3. Racially mixed people—Biography.] I. Title. II. Series: People in the news (San Diego, Calif.)
GV964.W66U73   1999
796.3352'092—dc21
[B]   98-50295
                                                                        CIP
                                                                         AC

Dedication

To my nephews Michael, Matthew, Ian, Mark, and T.R.
Here are a few seconds of the "fifteen minutes of fame"
everyone is supposed to enjoy during their lifetime.

Table of Contents

Foreword

FAME AND CELEBRITY are alluring. People are drawn to those who walk in fame's spotlight, whether they are known for great accomplishments or for notorious deeds. The lives of the famous pique public interest and attract attention, perhaps because their experiences seem in some ways so different from, yet in other ways so similar to, our own.

Newspapers, magazines, and television regularly capitalize on this fascination with celebrity by running profiles of famous people. For example, television programs such as *Entertainment Tonight* devote all of their programming to stories about entertainment and entertainers. Magazines such as *People* fill their pages with stories of the private lives of famous people. Even newspapers, newsmagazines, and television news frequently delve into the lives of well-known personalities. Despite the number of articles and programs, few provide more than a superficial glimpse at their subjects.

Lucent's People in the News series offers young readers a deeper look into the lives of today's newsmakers, the influences that have shaped them, and the impact they have had in their fields of endeavor and on other people's lives. The subjects of the series hail from many disciplines and walks of life. They include authors, musicians, athletes, political leaders, entertainers, entrepreneurs, and others who have made a mark on modern life and who, in many cases, will continue to do so for years to come.

These biographies are more than factual chronicles. Each book emphasizes the contributions, accomplishments, or deeds that have brought fame or notoriety to the individual and shows how that person has influenced modern life. Authors portray their subjects in a realistic, unsentimental light. For example, Bill Gates—the cofounder and chief executive officer of the software giant Microsoft—has been instrumental in making personal computers the most vital tool of the modern age. Few dispute his business savvy, his perseverance, or his technical expertise, yet critics say he is ruthless in his dealings with competitors and driven more by his desire to maintain Microsoft's dominance in the computer industry than by an interest in furthering technology.

In these books, young readers will encounter inspiring stories about real people who achieved success despite enormous obstacles. Oprah Winfrey—the most powerful, most watched, and wealthiest woman on television today—spent the first six years of her life in the care of her grandparents while her unwed mother sought work and a better life elsewhere. Her adolescence was colored by promiscuity, pregnancy at age fourteen, rape, and sexual abuse.

Each author documents and supports his or her work with an array of primary and secondary source quotations taken from diaries, letters, speeches, and interviews. All quotes are footnoted to show readers exactly how and where biographers derive their information and provide guidance for further research. The quotations enliven the text by giving readers eyewitness views of the life and accomplishments of each person covered in the People in the News series.

In addition, each book in the series includes photographs, annotated bibliographies, timelines, and comprehensive indexes. For both the casual reader and the student researcher, the People in the News series offers insight into the lives of today's newsmakers—people who shape the way we live, work, and play in the modern age.

Introduction

From Child Prodigy to Superstar

"PLEASE FORGIVE ME . . . but sometimes I get very emotional . . . when I talk about my son. My heart . . . fills with *so . . . much . . . joy . . .* when I realize . . . that this young man . . . is going to be able . . . to help so many people. He will *transcend* this game . . . and bring to the world . . . a humanitarianism . . . which has never been known before. The world will be a better place to live in . . . by virtue of his existence . . . and his presence. I acknowledge only a small part in that . . . in that I know that I was personally selected by God himself . . . to nurture this young man . . . and bring him to the point where he can make his contribution to humanity. This is my treasure. Please accept it . . . and use it wisely. . . . Thank you."[1]

His voice breaking with emotion, Earl Woods spoke those words in November 1996 at the Fred Haskins dinner to honor Eldrick "Tiger" Woods as the year's top collegiate golfer. Except for the brief reference to "this game," the tribute seemed more fitting for a world leader, religious figure, or great humanitarian than for a professional athlete.

Woods may be forgiven for being a father whose love and pride for his son overcame his sense of perspective, but his remarks go squarely to the central mystery that revolves around this sports superstar.

That mystery is not *how* Tiger became one of the world's great golfers but *why* he has been able to transcend the sport and capture the hearts and minds of so many millions of people around the world—men, women, and children of all ages, races, and walks of life who B. T. (Before Tiger) did not know a birdie from a bogey.

Golf's Child Prodigy

To start with, people are awed and intrigued by the legendlike tale of this golf prodigy—the infant who first learned to swing a club while sitting in a high chair watching his dad practice; the two-year-old who bested comedian Bob Hope in a putting contest on national television; the three-year-old who shot a score of 48 for nine holes; the youngest player, and first black, to win the U.S. Junior Amateur Championship at fifteen, the U.S. Amateur Championship at eighteen, and the Masters at twenty-one. The precociousness of Tiger's accomplishments, feats worthy of a fictional hero like Paul Bunyan or Pecos Bill, leaves people stunned.

Golf fans are equally enthralled with his personality in a sport that is mostly barren of charismatic stars. While playing, Tiger shows the ferocity of his animal namesake. He pumps his right arm in a savage uppercut to signify victory, glares menacingly when he misses a putt, and stalks the course like a predator, graceful but dangerous at the same time. His smile, one of

His hat turned comically to the side, this picture captures the lighter side of young Tiger Woods.

the biggest, sweetest ever flashed in sports, has captured the affection of millions of fans.

The world is also entranced by his racial mix. His father's heritage is black, Caucasian, and Native American, while his mother, Kultida, who is from Thailand, is of Thai and Chinese descent. Although his father says that in America any person with even one drop of black blood is considered black, Tiger coined the word *Cablinasian* to reflect his diverse ethnic makeup, a near-acronym of Caucasian (CA), black (BL), American Indian (IN), and Asian (ASIAN). Tiger considers himself to be one-fourth black, one-fourth Thai, one-fourth Chinese, one-eighth Native American, and one-eighth Caucasian.

People are fascinated that someone with Tiger's diverse ethnic heritage has become the premiere figure in golf, a sport traditionally dominated by whites, a sport in which, for far too long, blacks and other minorities were barred from even competing.

Tiger has become a hero not only to blacks and Asians, who joyfully claim him as one of their own, but to people of all races who appreciate that he is not only comfortable with his mixed heritage, but celebrates it. In America, a nation in which race is still a divisive issue, this achievement may be more important than any victory Tiger ever secures on the golf course.

Media Superstar

The power of today's mass media has helped Tiger become a cultural icon. The day after he turned professional in September 1996, television ads for golf equipment and apparel began bombarding hundreds of millions of people around the world with his smiling face. For nearly his entire life, newspapers, magazines, and television had been spreading the legend of Tiger Woods to the four corners of the planet. Like Michael (Jordan), Magic (Johnson), and (Muhammad) Ali before him, Tiger has achieved the cult status that allows him to be recognized by just a single name.

Sports agent Leigh Steinberg feels the world has only begun to feel his impact:

The slogan for this American Express ad could also be applied to Tiger Woods, who has a chance to do so many more important things in his life, both on and off a golf course.

Tiger has a chance to have an even broader appeal than Michael Jordan because we live in a time when communications [are] so instantaneous and so universal that a guy sitting on an island in the Pacific could have watched him win the Masters live. [He] could have the most profound impact inside and outside of sports of any athlete since Muhammad Ali.[2]

Maybe Earl Woods is right, after all.

Chapter 1

A Champion Made, Not Born

Earl Woods admits that in his son, Eldrick "Tiger" Woods, he has created a "beautiful monster." In *Training a Tiger: A Father's Guide to Raising a Winner in Both Golf and Life*, Woods relates his reaction the first time his son beat him at golf:

> There are two times that are the "first" time that Tiger beat me. On one occasion, we were playing a par-3 course called Heartwell in Long Beach [California]. Tiger was eight years old, and I hate to say it, but he did beat me, although I wasn't really trying my best, so I don't acknowledge it as a true defeat. It is still disputed today [between father and son], but I must admit that when he said, "Daddy, I beat you," they were the sweetest words I'd ever heard. In my record book Tiger first really beat me when he was eleven. I was trying my best, but he honestly whipped me. I haven't come close to beating him since and I never will. So parents be warned, you are creating a monster. But it is a beautiful monster . . . and you will be so proud and happy.[3]

However, more than just golf lessons from the time Tiger was an infant shaped his personality and his life. From the day Tiger was born December 30, 1975, in Cypress, California, a community near Los Angeles, both his parents sensed they had a special child, destined to accomplish great things.

Their conviction was reinforced when Kultida Woods, who raised her son as a Buddhist, took Tiger on a trip to her native

From the time Tiger was an infant, Earl Woods helped him develop his golf skills.

Thailand when he was nine years old. During the visit a Buddhist monk analyzed a chart she had kept on her son since his birth, in keeping with Thai custom. "He ask me did I ask God to give this boy Tiger to be born," she said. "I ask why? He say because this kid is special, like God send an angel to be born. He said this Tiger is special kid. The monk don't know about golf. The monk said it's like God send angel. He said Tiger going to be leader. If he go in the Army he be a four star general."[4]

At age nine, Tiger was already becoming famous for his precocious accomplishments in golf. He was successful at such an early age, in part, because his parents devoted their lives to him, sacrificing time and money to help him become a great golfer. Tiger himself believes the most important gift his parents gave him was an all-encompassing sense of love and security, which is symbolized by his little-used first name:

> When I was growing up, my parents loved to remind me
> that I was named Eldrick for a special reason. The "E" at
> the beginning represents Earl and the "K" at the end

stands for Kultida. My mother said she wanted their initials to encompass my name so that I would always be surrounded by my parents. Thankfully, that has been the case. I am the product of their careful guidance and discipline. The many ideals and lessons I've learned from my mother and father define who I am and make me proud of who I am.[5]

Tiger's comment appears in the foreword to the book his father wrote about how he taught his son to play golf. But the reason Earl Woods felt compelled to introduce Tiger to this game at such an early age goes back to his own past, one which included brushes with racism.

Earl Woods's Early Life

Earl Woods grew up in Manhattan, Kansas, the sixth child of Maude and Miles Woods. His father died when he was eleven and his mother when he was thirteen, leaving Earl and his siblings to

Tiger and Cosmic Intervention

Many parents feel their children are special but the belief of Earl and Kultida Woods that their son was destined for greatness goes far deeper than that. Both claim Tiger was born for a "purpose" and that their lives were guided by fate to produce a child who would have a huge impact on the world. Tim Rosaforte explains this belief in *Tiger Woods: The Makings of a Champion*.

> Earl, who grew up a Presbyterian in Manhattan, Kansas, believes that Tiger is a chosen one. So does Tiger's mom, Tida. They believe their son was put on this Earth with a greater purpose than just winning golf tournaments. Earl and Tida Woods also believe that some of the people who cross Tiger's path are also part of a divine fate. Says Earl, "A divine power has put him here for a purpose. This isn't just my analysis and my idea. There are other people who have been blessed to be a part of this, who have in retrospect gone back and reviewed their lives and come to the same conclusions . . . that they were individually prepared for the moment that their life intersected with Tiger's life. It has happened over and over again, and it will happen in the future. Other people will also be prepared, and they will interface with his life when it is time."

Earl Woods proudly displays a copy of his first book, Training A Tiger, *in which he explains how he taught Tiger to play golf.*

be raised by his oldest sister, Hattie. The Woods family struggled financially when he was growing up. "I am not proud of it, but I distinctly remember our family receiving Thanksgiving Day baskets from the Rotary Club," he said. "But in my mind, we were not poor. I didn't grow up feeling inferior to anyone, at least not in my mind. Our personal worth remained rich and stable within the confines of our family, which was firmly headed by my mother."[6]

Earl's father had dreamed that his son would one day play baseball for the Kansas City Monarchs of the Negro League. Until 1947, when Jackie Robinson broke the color line with the Brooklyn Dodgers, blacks were barred from playing in the major leagues. In high school Earl starred as a catcher for an integrated American Legion team but when family members came out to watch him, they had to suffer along with Earl when fans shouted racial taunts. Woods remembers:

> It wasn't always easy for them, because they would be the only blacks in the entire stadium. They endured a lot to support me. As the catcher, I was right there in front

of the whole crowd, an easy target for countless bigots who didn't hesitate to hurl the "n" word all the time. Yet my sisters and my brother-in-law [Jesse Spearman] had to be cool and composed amidst the racial slurs and other denigrating comments from the crowd.[7]

Earl's talent earned him the opportunity to play for the Monarchs when he graduated from high school. But he was torn about what to do because his mother, who valued education above everything else, had dreamed of his going to college. Her ambition prevailed, and Earl went to Kansas State University on a baseball scholarship, majoring in sociology and minoring in psychology while becoming the first black athlete in what was then known as the Big Seven Conference. But he still had to put up with racism. In addition to taunts from bigoted fans, during road trips Woods often could not eat in the same restaurants or stay in the same hotels as his teammates.

While in college Woods joined the Reserve Officer Training Corps (ROTC), and after graduating in 1954 he entered the army as a second lieutenant. His first assignment was teaching a military history course at City College of New York; he then served in Germany, had two tours of duty in Vietnam as a member of the Green Berets, and was also stationed in Thailand. It was during the Vietnam War that he met Vuong Dang Phong, a colonel in the South Vietnamese army.

During the Vietnam War, Woods and Phong fought side-by-side through many battles. Each saved the other's life a number of times and Woods began calling Phong "Tiger" for his bravery. It was a nickname Woods would pass on to his son in honor of his friend, who died in a North Vietnamese reeducation camp after the war.

"That guy was so brave, I decided my son's nickname would be Tiger," Woods says. "[Phong] was the first cosmic intersection in the life of a kid who hadn't been born yet, a kid who would touch the world."[8]

Kultida Woods

The day before Woods entered the service he was married; he and his wife, Barbara, eventually had three children: sons Earl

The First Tiger

After Earl Woods left South Vietnam in 1971 following his second tour of duty, he never saw Vuong Dang Phong again and never knew what happened to the man he revered as the first "Tiger."

But in 1996 *Golf Digest* writer Tom Callahan visited Vietnam to find out what became of the war comrade who had saved Earl's life several times and inspired him to nickname his own son "Tiger." Callahan, admitting that he doubted at first if the story about the war comrades was true, discovered Phong had died in a North Vietnamese reeducation camp in 1976, just eight months after Tiger Woods was born. He also learned that Phong's widow and three children had later moved to the United States and were living in Tacoma, Washington.

Before the story was published in October 1997, Callahan let Woods read what happened to his friend. "I cried like a baby for two days," Earl said. When Woods called Tiger with the news, his son tried to comfort him. "Tiger kept saying, 'I know, I know,'" his father said. "His psyche is full of Tiger lore."

The magazine arranged an emotional meeting with Phong's widow and two children at Tiger's home in Orlando, Florida. For the young golfer, it was a chance to come face to face with the reality behind the nickname he has made world famous.

"I always knew there was another Tiger," he said. "I didn't know him as Tiger Phong. I just knew him as Tiger One."

Dennison Jr. and Kevin Dale and daughter Royce Renay. The couple was unhappy from the start, but Woods says he stayed in the marriage for the sake of his children. Woods admits that some of their marital problems stemmed from the long periods he was away from home on military assignments. During his second tour of duty in Vietnam, August 15, 1970, to August 13, 1971, he decided to divorce.

During a tour of duty in Thailand after his first marriage had fallen apart he met the woman who would become Tiger's mother. It was a meeting he feels was preordained. Kultida was a receptionist at the military base in Bangkok where Woods was stationed; he asked her to go out with him and she said yes. The couple had to overcome cultural differences in their relationship, including a misunderstanding that nearly ruined their first date. In his biography of Tiger Woods, John Strege relates this comical mishap:

They agreed to meet at eight. He was under the impression it was eight that night, while she thought it was the following morning. "Thai girls not go out at night," she [later] said. That night, Earl waited patiently, then impatiently, until it was apparent she was not going to show. He was convinced he had been stood up. The following morning, when Earl failed to show, Kultida was sure she had been stood up. A proud, defiant woman who does not take rejection lightly, she and a friend went on a manhunt. When she found Earl, she said tersely, "We had a date." "Yeah, last night," Earl said. "We still have date," she insisted. It was a holy day and she asked that he take her to the Temple of the Reclining Buddha. "So I took her," Earl said.[9]

Kultida had been raised in a boarding school after her parents separated when she was five. It was unusual for a Thai woman like Kultida, well-off and educated, to date an American serviceman, especially a black. Moreover, Woods was about twenty years older. But Earl and Kultida fell in love despite their differences and after he returned home from his assignment in Thailand, Tida joined him in New York in 1973 and they were married. Woods explains:

> She trusted me, and eventually came to the United States against the will of her mother and most of her family. It took a lot of guts and faith in me for her to do that. And she was greatly ostracized by some of her people for her decision. But she certainly got her revenge: When she returned to Thailand many years later [in 1997] as the mother of Tiger Woods, she was suddenly transformed into a heroine. Nearly 1,000 well-wishers greeted Tiger at the airport when he arrived for a tournament. How quickly fame and fortune affect the attitudes of people.[10]

His First Family

Critics of Earl Woods have accused him of ignoring his first three children after Tiger was born. In interviews Woods never talked about them and in his first book, *Training a Tiger*, he

Kultida Woods has always been at Tiger's side, loving him, cheering him on, and teaching him lessons about life more important than anything he could learn on a golf course.

appeared to dismiss his first attempt at fatherhood as merely good training that would make him a better father to Tiger.

But in his second book, *Playing Through: Straight Talk on Hard Work, Big Dreams, and Adventures with Tiger,* Woods answered that criticism by writing about his other children. Woods maintains he never put them out of his life and that in 1974, when he retired from the service as a lieutenant colonel, he kept his promise to move back to California to be near them.

Hired by McDonnell Douglas to negotiate contracts in their rocket program, Earl and Tida Woods lived in a condominium in the Los Angeles suburb of Los Alamitos for a year before buying a home in Cypress. While they were still living in Los Alamitos, Woods's oldest son, Earl Jr., who had just turned eighteen, moved in with the couple. His other two children also lived with Earl and Tida from the ages of eighteen to twenty-one.

However, even in his second book, Earl Woods still claims that God gave him his first three children mainly to prepare him to raise Tiger:

As with so many things in my life, I feel now that my first marriage was a test. The Lord said, "Let's give this guy a boy and see how he handles it. Give him another one. Well, let's give him a girl and see how he handles that." Then he put me through the trials and tribulations of any unhappy marriage. He was testing me, always testing me and preparing me. By the time I was in a position to re-marry, I was better prepared to handle children. And that's what he had in mind. I can see it all clearly now.[11]

A Tiger Cub

By the time of Tiger's birth, his father was already a fanatical golfer. Earl Woods was forty-two when he played golf for the first time, taking up the game after a friend dared him to a match at an army base in Fort Dix, New Jersey. Woods played poorly, shooting 92 for seventeen holes, and was angry afterward that his friend bragged about beating him. A proud athlete who had excelled in many sports, Woods decided to challenge his buddy to a rematch. He worked furiously to improve and shot 84 to beat his friend by four strokes.

"It was then I decided that if I ever had another child, he or she would be exposed to the game earlier than I had been and along came Tiger," he says. "By the time he was born, I was nearly a scratch player, so God's game plan was already in ef-fect. I had been properly trained and was ready to go. I took over new ground in starting Tiger at an early age and developed teaching techniques that were easily communicated to him."[12]

The development of one of golf's greatest players began in-nocently enough in the garage of the family home in Cypress. Realizing he had not spent enough time with his first three chil-dren, Woods wanted to be with his new son as much as possible. So when Tiger was just six months old, Woods began taking him into the garage so Tiger could be with him while he practiced hitting golf balls into a net.

Tiger's father was surprised that the infant would sit so qui-etly and watch so intently, often while eating a bowl of rice ce-real and mashed bananas. But his father's amazement over his son's intense concentration was nothing compared with his

Golf Terminology

As a youngster, Tiger Woods had to master not only the game of golf but the special words golfers use to describe their game. Here are definitions of some of the key terms in golf.

Par: The number of strokes a golfer should need to get the ball in the hole in regulation. Golf courses have par-3, par-4, and par-5 holes. Par-3 holes are the shortest, usually under 200 yards, while par-4 holes are longer, up to 500 yards, and par-5 holes are generally longer than 500 yards. Golfers are allowed two putts for each hole, which means they are expected to reach a par-3 green in one shot, a par-4 in two, and a par-5 in three swings.

Birdie: A score that is one under par, such as a three on a par-4.

Bogey: A score that is one over par, such as a five on a par-4.

Eagle: A score that is two under par, such as a three on a par-5.

Hole-in-One: A shot from the tee-off area that goes into the hole.

Match Play: A tournament in which two golfers play against each other to win individual holes. There are usually several rounds of elimination to determine the overall winner. In match play, a golfer wins when he or she is ahead by more holes than there are left to play. A winning 2-up score, for example, means a golfer was up two holes with only one left to play. If the golfers finish in a tie, they keep playing until one player wins a hole. If both golfers tie on a hole, neither wins and the hole is considered "halved."

Medal Play: Also called stroke play; a tournament in which the winner is the golfer with the lowest score over a predetermined number of holes.

Par-3 Course: Courses that have shorter holes, usually all par-3s, and are about 2,500 yards long.

Regulation Course: Longer courses, between 6,000 and 7,000 yards or more, that have a combination of par-3, par-4, and par-5 holes. The most common regulation par for such a course is 72, the total of the par for all the holes.

reaction to what Tiger did one day when he was just ten months old. Woods had sat down to rest when Tiger climbed out of his high chair, put a ball in place on the practice mat, grabbed a putter his father had cut down for him, and executed a swing that was a carbon copy of his dad's.

"I was flabbergasted. I almost fell off my chair," says Woods. "It was the most frightening thing I had ever seen." He then ran into the house, shouting to his wife, "We have a genius on our hands."[13]

Chapter 2

Early Success and Fame

ALTHOUGH EARL WOODS claims he never set out to make Tiger a great golfer, he had vowed that his son would have every chance to play a game blacks generally have not had the opportunity to learn, either through a lack of money or racist policies that excluded them from courses and golf programs. "I was a black kid and golf was played at the country club—end of story," Woods says in explaining why he did not start golfing until he was forty-two years old. "But I told myself that somehow my son would get a chance to play golf early in life." [14]

Woods believes there had never been a great black golfer before Tiger because so few blacks had played the game from an early age. "See, this is the first intuitive black golfer ever raised in the United States," Woods said years later. "Before, black kids grew up with basketball or baseball from the time they could walk. The game became part of them from the beginning. But they always learned golf too late. Not Tiger. Tiger knew how to swing a golf club before he could walk." [15]

Infant Golfer

Earl Woods gave his son a cut-down putter when Tiger was seven months old, and it quickly became the infant's favorite toy. Tiger dragged it with him wherever he roamed in his walker. "When most kids are in those circular walkers, you give them a rattle," says Earl Woods. "He had a putter." [16]

Tiger began to practice with his father in the garage. When he was eighteen months old, Earl took him to a driving range for the first time to hit balls. A few months before his third birthday Tiger played his first hole, a 410-yard par 4 on a golf course

Earl Woods and Tiger in 1995 when he debuted in the prestigious Masters Tournament in Augusta, Georgia.

owned by the U.S. Navy known as the Destroyer Course. (As a retired army officer, Woods was accorded playing privileges at courses owned by any branch of the U.S. armed forces.) Tiger's first recorded score was an 11—eight shots to reach the green and three putts to get the ball in the hole.

Tiger continued practicing and began playing the navy courses while still wearing diapers. At age three he won a pitch, putt, and drive competition against kids ages ten and eleven and one day before his fourth birthday Tiger shot 48 for nine holes at a navy course. True, his father allowed Tiger to tee up the ball in the fairway, but it was a remarkable accomplishment, nonetheless.

When people saw the minigolfer smashing shots and sinking putts, they would ask him how he got so good. "Practice, practice, practice, oooh," [17] was his reply. The child's response was all the more charming because Tiger, like many youngsters, had trouble saying his "Rs"—the word "practice" came out "pwactice." His father believes the "oooh" came from something Tiger heard on television.

When his proud mother telephoned a Los Angeles television station to brag about Tiger, sportscaster Jim Hill did a story about the precocious golfer which led to Tiger's debut on national television. On October 6, 1978, two months shy of his third birthday, Tiger appeared on the *Mike Douglas Show* to display the talents that were already making the pint-size golfer a celebrity in California.

Douglas, host of the daytime television talk show, told comedian Bob Hope "there's someone here to challenge you" in golf. An avid golfer who hosted a professional tournament, Hope was stunned when little Tiger, clad in shorts, wearing a red cap, and with his small bag of cut-down clubs slung across his shoulder, strode confidently onto the stage. Hope and actor Jimmy Stewart watched in amazement as the two-year-old teed up several balls and smashed them to the back of the stage with his sawed-off driver. They could not believe the smoothness and power of the toddler's swing.

When Douglas told Hope he would be putting against Tiger in a contest, the comedian looked down at his tiny opponent and quipped, "You got any money?"[18] The laughter from the audience soon turned to applause as Tiger made his putts to upstage Hope.

The legend of this wondrously athletic child was beginning to grow.

Rudy Duran and Heartwell Park

When Tiger was four, the navy courses he had been playing with his father started enforcing a minimum-age policy of ten years for children. His mother searched for a course that would accept Tiger and found Heartwell Golf Park, a par-3 course in Long Beach. (A par-3 course is entirely composed of shorter holes, most of them less than one hundred yards, which Earl and Tida felt would be easier for Tiger to play than regulation courses, in which some holes are longer than 500 yards.) Rudy Duran, the head pro at the course, was skeptical of giving such a small child playing privileges but he only had to watch Tiger hit seven shots to realize the child was good enough. "He had talent oozing out of his fingertips,"[19] Duran says.

Duran became Tiger's first professional teacher, something Earl Woods realized his son needed to improve. For Duran it was the chance of a lifetime to coach a great talent: "He was definitely a golf genius. He had a natural swing and ability to learn that was incredible. It's hard for me to describe how good he was on that first day. But over the next [six] years it was really obvious that this guy was, at that time, one of the best golfers I've ever seen. By the time he was six years old he was, to me, like a shrunken touring pro."[20]

Unlike most youngsters, Tiger was not easily distracted when playing golf. Duran says that though Tiger enjoyed chasing the frogs he would see on the course, he would ignore them when he had a club in his hands: "When Tiger saw a frog, he would continue playing. He would wait until the end of his round. Then he would say, 'Let's find that frog!'"[21]

At age four Tiger still used only a putter, driver, and seven iron, which were cut down to accommodate his size, but the next year he got his first full set of clubs. Duran began to refine Tiger's swing, teaching him how to hit the ball longer and with more accuracy as well as how to use all of his new clubs.

"Tiger Pars"

In golf each hole is assigned a number for par but even though Tiger was already a good golfer mechanically, it was impossible for him to make par because he was not strong enough to hit the ball very far. To build up Tiger's confidence, Duran set what he called "Tiger pars" for each hole based on his strength and ability. The first course "Tiger par" for Heartwell Park was 67, eight strokes higher than par for everyone else. At age five Tiger was already shooting scores in the 90s on par-72 golf courses, a score beyond many adult golfers, but Duran and his father still kept his confidence up by assigning him "Tiger pars."

When Tiger was five, his father used his son's appearance on the network television show *That's Incredible* to teach him a valuable lesson. Another guest on the show was a young girl about eleven who was a weightlifter. She managed to lift hosts John Davidson, Fran Tarkenton, and Cathy Lee on a special harness that had been prepared for her display of strength. Woods looked at his son and asked him, "Can you do that?" Tiger answered, "No, Daddy." Woods then explained to Tiger, "She is a special person. She is a special person in weightlifting. You are special in golf. And there are a lot of special people in the world in whatever they do. You are one of them. Do you understand that?" Tiger said, "Yes, Daddy."[22]

Woods wanted his son to realize not only that he had a special talent, but that other people had special gifts that he did not have so he would not feel superior just because he was good at golf. When Tiger was interviewed during the show, he said that when he grew up, "I want to win all the big tournaments, the major ones. I hope to play well when I get older, beat all the pros."[23]

Unsportsmanlike Conduct

By age six Tiger was able to drive the ball 126 yards, amazing for someone that small, and had already begun to develop his fierce appetite for winning. Playing golf with club pro Stewart Reed, Tiger managed to beat him over the first nine holes. But when Reed pulled away on the second nine, the young golfer sulked about his defeat and refused to shake Reed's hand at the end of the match. Unsportsmanlike conduct was something his mother would not tolerate. "You're only six, he is a pro, you can't beat a pro," she scolded him. Tida also told him, "You must be a sportsman, win or lose."[24]

Tida was Tiger's main disciplinarian as well as the teacher of many important lessons about life. Once when tennis star John McEnroe was playing a televised match, Tida pointed out his reputation of acting like a spoiled brat and told Tiger: "I don't want the one and only one [of her children] to grow up spoiled. 'Watch John McEnroe,' I tell Tiger. Never that. I don't like that. I'll not have my reputation as a parent ruined by that."[25]

Another time after Tiger had made a bad shot in a tournament, he angrily slammed his club down on his golf bag. Tida responded by asking the tournament director to give her son a two-shot penalty for unsportsmanlike conduct. She then asked Tiger, "Who made the bad shot? Whose fault is it? If you want to hit something, hit yourself in the head."[26]

*Kultida Woods and Sarah Ferguson, the former duchess of York, watch
Tiger play in the Byron Nelson Classic in May 1997.*

Although Duran was now teaching Tiger the mechanics of the
game, Earl Woods was working to strengthen his son psychologically. When Tiger was six, he gave him a motivational tape that
played soft music while a voice spoke positive psychological mes-
sages such as: "I believe in me. . . . I smile at obstacles. . . . My
decisions are strong! . . . I do it with all my heart! . . . I will my own
destiny!" They helped give Tiger confidence to play golf even
when things went wrong.

When he was seven, Earl put Tiger through what he called
the Woods Finishing School to prepare him for match play,
which can be more demanding psychologically and emotionally
than medal play. In medal play, in which a field of golfers try to
shoot the lowest score over a set number of holes, the competition is mainly the golfer against the course itself and contending
players might never see each other. But in match play, two
golfers battle head-to-head to win individual holes. In this type
of competition some players try to rattle their opponents with
unsportsmanlike tactics. Woods explains his demonstration:

A Mother's Influence

Earl Woods has been criticized for trying to grab the lion's share of publicity and credit for turning his son into one of the finest golfers who ever lived. But in *Playing Through: Straight Talk on Hard Work, Big Dreams, and Adventures with Tiger,* he writes about the vital role Tiger's mother, Kultida, played in their son's development both as a golfer and a person. Following are two excerpts from *Playing Through* in which Earl praises Tiger's mother.

Tida took to motherhood like a duck to water, and she generally does not receive enough credit for the rearing of Tiger. I believe the groundwork for a child comes from the mother, because she spends so much time with the youngster in the formative years. In so many respects, Tiger was raised as an Asian child, not as an American. The way Tiger was taught to respect his parents and other adults, to rely on his instincts and feelings, to be unselfish and generous . . . these are all tenets of Asian philosophy and culture that he has embraced.

• • • • •

Tida should receive great credit for assuring that Tiger stayed on target when it came to schoolwork. She had a very simple rule: "No schoolwork, no golf." And Tiger bought into this completely. Her Asian cultural influence on Tiger's upbringing was critical in his quick maturation. Tida always preached humility, determination, respect, spirituality, honesty and diligence in her daily interaction with Tiger. The devotion between Tiger and his mother underscores his insistence not to deny his racial heritage. To this day he wears a heavy gold chain with the replica of a gold Buddha around his neck, a symbol of the Buddhist religion he embraces. And you might say Tiger continues to wear his feelings about his mother on his sleeve.

I pulled every nasty, dirty, obnoxious trick on my own son, week after week. I dropped a bag of clubs at the impact of his swing. I imitated a crow's voice while he was stroking a putt. I would cough as he was taking the club back. I would say, "Don't hit it in the water." Those were the *nice* things I did. In other words, I played with his mind and don't forget, he was not permitted to say a word. Sometimes he got so angry with me that he would stop his club on the downswing inches before impact, turn, and glare at me because I had dropped a set of clubs on the ground. He would grit his teeth and roll his eyes, and the only response he got was, "Don't look at me. Are you going to hit the ball or not?"[27]

Earl believes the result of that harsh education was the supreme confidence Tiger now shows while playing, one of his greatest strengths. "Let me tell you something," he told Tiger when he "graduated" from his finishing school. "I promise you the rest of your life you will never meet another person as mentally tough as you are."[28]

The Child Genius Excels

The combination of golf instruction from Duran, lessons in life and living from Tida, and Earl's psychological toughening helped Tiger blossom as a young golfer. He had been playing competitively since the age of four in Southern California Junior Golf Association events and his first victory had come in just his fourth tournament, at Yorba Linda Country Club, when he beat a golfer six years older than himself.

As is often true in sports involving very young competitors, Tiger's mother was an important part of his success. Kultida rousted young Tiger out of bed as early as 4 A.M. so they could travel to tournaments or to practice. Tiger often fell asleep in the car, his head on his favorite pillow while his mom drove. Like other mothers, Tida became a volunteer scorekeeper and rules interpreter for tournaments her son entered.

In 1983, when Tiger was eight years old, he won his first Optimist International Junior World Championship for golfers ages eight to ten. When he won that first title at Presidio Park Golf Course in San Diego, California, Tiger was only four feet, six inches tall and weighed seventy-five pounds, but he could drive the ball 170 yards and was a fierce competitor. "Tiger took winning as a given," his father says. "The little guy just knew intuitively how good he was."[29] Tiger also won five more age-group Optimist titles at the ages of nine, twelve, thirteen, fourteen, and fifteen.

In August 1989, when he was thirteen, Tiger faced the biggest challenge of his young life when he played for the first time in the Insurance Youth Golf Classic National at the Texarkana Country Club in Texarkana, Arkansas. In one round the young golfers were paired with professionals; Tiger's group drew John Daly, a prodigiously long hitter who has won the U.S. Open and British Open.

After Woods shot three under par for the first nine holes, two shots better than Daly, the stunned pro was heard to mutter, "I can't let this thirteen-year-old beat me."[30] Daly birdied three of the last four holes to defeat Tiger 70 to 72. Woods finished second overall in the tournament to Justin Leonard, a young golfer who in 1997 would win the British Open.

Racism

Tiger Woods grew up knowing he was special because of his gift for golf. But he was soon forced to realize that some children would consider him different simply because of the color of his skin. This bitter lesson came on his first day of kindergarten in September 1981 at a school that had few minority students. A group of older boys, all of them white, tied Tiger to a tree, taunted him with racial slurs such as "monkey" and "nigger," and threw rocks at him. The offenders were caught and punished, but Tiger has never forgotten the incident.

Tiger's initiation into the harsh world faced by many minorities reflected the harassment Earl and Tida had to endure when they moved into their home in Cypress before he was born. Biographer John Strege explains the couple's reception, which occurred while Tida was pregnant:

> Earl and Kultida put out a welcome mat, but the neighbors hardly reciprocated. The Woods home became a target of open bigotry, driven in part by the then widely accepted belief that property values declined in neighborhoods when black families moved in. Their housewarming gifts were windfall limes from neighborhood trees delivered as fastballs and aimed at windows. In a matter of weeks, arms throwing limes gave way to guns shooting BBs, an escalation in hostilities that might have made other families start packing. The green beret was not inclined to retreat, however. The Woodses stood their ground, and when it became apparent that they intended to stay, a cease-fire emerged.[31]

Tiger believes the decision not to allow him to continue playing at navy courses when he was four was also based on

Effects of Racism on Tiger

Many children have nightmares in which a monster stalks them. For Tiger Woods, that "monster" was racism. His experiences at an early age taught him that some people would reject him solely because of the color of his skin, the shape of his features, the texture of his hair, whether he met them on a golf course or in a kindergarten class.

As a reporter for the *Orange County Register*, John Strege wrote many stories about Tiger while he was growing up. In *Tiger: A Biography of Tiger Woods*, Strege discusses how racism affected Tiger.

> Despite his relative silence on the subject as an adult, Tiger's experience with racial bigotry had a great impact on him psychologically and socially throughout his childhood. He had had his nightmares, as kids typically do, except that the terror that haunted his sleep was more enduring and not likely to go away when he awoke. When he was eight, he began dreaming that he was playing golf in the South and that he was the target of an assassin. The nightmares occurred for about two years, but as he continued to develop as a golfer, his self-esteem grew, enabling him to handle the bigotry directed toward him. "It's their racism, not mine," Tiger says. It is their problem, not his. "I've been able to convince him there isn't anything he can do about it," Earl said. "It's been an abiding principle I've taught him that you don't worry about things over which you have no control."

racism. In 1990 Tiger was again allowed to play the navy courses because he was older but during a junior golf tournament that year he said: "They don't like me at my home course. They tried to shut me out. I think it's my skin color. The pro let me play when I was four, but the members got mad because I was beating them."[32]

Racism is something that Tiger has had to deal with his entire life. He learned to handle it by accepting some advice from his mother: "Racism is not your problem, it's theirs," she told him. "Just play your game."[33]

Chapter 3

The Greatest Amateur Golfer Ever

By the time Tiger Woods was eleven years old, he was already well known for his feats as a toddler and his many victories as a junior golfer. But even at that tender age, Tiger was considering his long-range goals in the sport he loved. It was then that Tiger decided to chase the records set by Jack Nicklaus, the golfer nicknamed the "Golden Bear" who is generally considered the greatest ever to play the game by golf historians, sportswriters, and fans of the sport.

Tiger made a three-column chart: The first column listed major championships including the four professional tournaments that make up the grand slam of golf, the Masters, U.S. Open, British Open, and PGA (Professional Golfers' Association) Championship; the second showed how old Nicklaus was when he first won each of them; the last one, topped by Tiger's name, was blank. Tiger then put a picture of Nicklaus on the chart and hung it on his bedroom wall.

"I wanted to be the youngest player ever to win the majors. Nicklaus was my hero, and I thought it would be great to accomplish all the things he did earlier than he accomplished them," Tiger says.[34]

Family Life

By age fourteen Tiger had collected so many trophies that his family home was beginning to resemble a shrine. His development as a golfer had become the focus of family life.

Many people consider Jack Nicklaus the greatest golfer in history.

"To our family, the big picture became Tiger's extraordinary ability, and how to nurture it," Earl Woods says.

The reality was that Tiger's early golf career was going to be costly, and on our relatively modest income, it was going to take some sacrifices and creative financing so that he could continue to compete, learn and grow. Of course, we were more than willing to sacrifice our personal and economic situations so that Tiger could do what he needed to do. We weren't necessarily sacrificing so that he could become a professional golfer; we just wanted to be there for our son and to facilitate his happiness. And golf was most certainly making him happy.[35]

Family life was dictated by Tiger's golf schedule. "For most families, summer and holidays meant vacations, togetherness," Woods says. "To us, summers and holidays were filled with tournaments. At Christmastime, I would travel with Tiger to Miami for the Junior Invitational Golf Tournament. On Thanksgiving Day, we would go to Tucson, Arizona. We spent Easter at the Woodlands Tournament in Texas. The hardest part was that Tida couldn't even go with us; we couldn't afford the traveling expense of two parents."[36]

Woods estimates it cost $25,000 to $30,000 a year to send Tiger to tournaments across the country and even overseas so he could develop as a golfer. Even as a youngster, Tiger understood the financial sacrifices and wanted to repay his parents. When he was ten years old Tiger asked his father, "Daddy, do you think when I turn pro you could live off one-hundred-thousand dollars a year?" Earl Woods turned to him and said, "Let me think about it. The tab is going up every week." [37]

The results of those sacrifices were impressive: In 1987 Tiger entered and won more than 30 junior tournaments. When he was thirteen he won his fourth Optimist International Junior World title, one more than any previous champion including pro golfing stars Corey Pavin, Nick Price, and Scott Simpson. By age sixteen he had captured 6 junior world titles, triumphed in more than 130 local and national junior tournaments, and competed in Paris, France, at age fourteen in the Southern California–France Junior Cup.

Although golf was Tiger's great passion, he had many other interests while growing up. Tida always made him finish his homework before he could practice golf, and as a result he earned good grades in school and graduated from Anaheim Western High School with a 3.79 grade-point average. A fine all-around athlete, in his first year in junior high school Tiger ran cross-country and as a junior at Western ran track in the 400-meter event, achieving a best time of 52 seconds. "Tiger is a beautiful runner," says his proud father. "If you think he has a beautiful golf swing, you should see him run." [38]

A Normal Kid

Like other kids his age, Tiger also watched television, played video games, listened to music, and hung out with his friends. "Hey, I had a normal childhood," Tiger once said. "I did the same things every kid did. I studied and went to the mall. I was addicted to TV wrestling, rap music and 'The Simpsons.' I got into trouble and got out of it. I loved my parents and obeyed what they told me." [39]

Earl Woods never forced Tiger to practice. "Well, quit," he would tell Tiger when his son was not in the mood for golf. "Jump on your bicycle and go over and see your friend Michael." Tiger would take off two days to play Nintendo or Ping-Pong with friends but he would always return to golf. "By the third day he would be back around the house, hitting golf shots all over the place. By the fourth day he was back on the golf course,"[40] Woods says.

His golfing ability made him a celebrity at an early age. His first appearance in *Sports Illustrated*, the weekly bible of sports, came in the magazine's September 24, 1990, issue. The brief caption next to his picture in the "Faces in the Crowd" section read: "CYPRESS CALIF: Tiger, 14, shot a two-under par 286 for 72 holes to win a national youth golf tournament at Ridglea Country Club in Fort Worth. He has also won five Junior World titles, including the Optimist International in San Diego last July."[41]

As a freshman at Anaheim Western High School, Tiger won twenty-seven of twenty-nine tournaments and as a senior in 1993 received the Dial Award as the national high school male athlete of the year. Tiger was already seeking goals that were far beyond high school golf, however. After all, he was already winning national championships and competing against professional golfers.

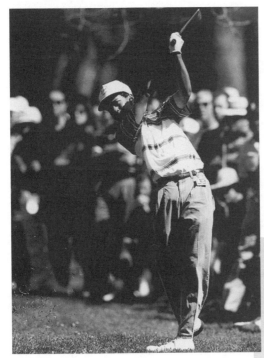

In 1992, when Tiger Woods was just 16, he appeared in the Los Angeles Open and became the youngest player to ever compete in a PGA tournament.

Team Tiger

Earl Woods headed the group of advisers and trainers who guided his son's quest for golfing greatness. He had retired from McDonnell Douglas in 1988 at age fifty-six to be free full-time to accompany Tiger to tournaments. Two years earlier John Anselmo, a teaching pro at Meadowlark Golf Course in Long Beach, had become his new swing instructor. "I saw so much rhythm and balance even when he was ten," Anselmo said. "I was awed by it. I knew at the time he was special. It's like it's destiny. It's so exciting to have been a part of the Tiger team." [42]

Anselmo changed Tiger's swing plane to accommodate his growing body. Tiger had finally begun his adolescent growth spurt. At age thirteen, Tiger was five-foot-six and weighed 107 pounds but a year later he had grown three more inches, gained 13 pounds, and was regularly shooting two under par 68 on the 6,820-yard, par-72 navy course. He was also becoming known for how far he could drive the ball despite his youth and still relatively small stature.

The final member of the team was Jay Brunza, a retired navy captain and clinical psychologist. Brunza, who had previously helped athletes at the U.S. Naval Academy learn to concentrate better to improve their performance, began working with Tiger. Brunza taught him mental tricks to increase his concentration and hypnotized Tiger to instill some of his lessons. He even taught the young golfer how to hypnotize himself to get the same results.

Brunza is credited with helping Tiger develop his almost Zen-like concentration, which allows him to focus on every shot. "In golf," Tiger says, "you have to concentrate like this!" Tiger snaps his fingers to show how quickly golfers must regain their focus after a bad shot or distraction so they can hit their next shot cleanly. "My father and I call it zoning. If you mishit a shot, hit it out of bounds, put it in the water, you have to get your focus back. You've got to start thinking ahead, don't look behind." [43]

This amazing ability to stay mentally and emotionally focused has helped Tiger come from behind to win many tournaments. In 1991, when Tiger captured his first U.S. Junior Amateur title at age fifteen, he trailed by three holes in the final round. Some players would have panicked but Tiger kept his composure, tying the match on the final hole and winning the first playoff hole to become the youngest and first black junior champion. Those two modifiers—"youngest" and "first black"—would be tacked on to Tiger's name again and again in the years ahead.

In 1992 Tiger became the first player to win the prestigious Junior Amateur title two years in a row, and in 1993 he won it a third time. In both 1992 and 1993 Tiger staged dramatic rallies to come from behind to win; in 1992 he was two holes back with six holes to play and in 1993 two down with two holes left, which meant he had to win both to win the tournament. Tiger birdied both of the final holes in 1993 even though he mishit his drive on the eighteenth, leaving him in a sand trap forty yards from the green. "I'm thinking he'll be lucky to get it on the green, and he knocks it to within ten feet," said his opponent, Ryan Armour, sixteen. "How good is that?"[44] Tiger made the birdie putt to square the match and won the title with a par on the first extra hole.

The U.S. Amateur Championship

His Junior Amateur titles qualified him for the U.S. Amateur Championship, which is open to golfers of any age, but he did not fare as well when he stepped up against older competition. In 1991 he shot 78 and 74 in the medal rounds, failing to make the cut for match play, but the next two years finished among the top thirty-two after advancing to match competition. In the 1993 U.S. Amateur, Tiger was eliminated in the second round by Paul Page of Great Britain by a score of 2-and-1. The score meant Page was two holes ahead with just one hole to play, so Tiger could not win.

Page, however, would be the last player to beat Woods in a competition run by the United States Golf Association, mainly because after the tournament Claude "Butch" Harmon Jr. became his new coach and helped make Tiger a much better player. Harmon, whose father, Claude, won the 1948 Masters, is one of the game's top teachers; he had come to the tournament to watch Tiger. His addition to Team Tiger would be key in enabling Tiger to reach his full potential. Harmon had already helped Australian Greg Norman tame his swing and become the top-ranked player in the world.

In Tiger, Harmon saw a player who could generate a lot of club head speed, which is necessary for power, but who was inconsistent because of a loose swing and big hip turn. Harmon widened Tiger's stance for greater stability, increased the arc at the top of his backswing, reduced his hip turn, and polished other fundamentals.

Harmon found Tiger an eager, willing student. "At this point he didn't have so much of the ego of Greg Norman, a proven champion," Harmon said. "You had a young man with some raw talent that you were really molding. He's like a sponge, he just soaks up knowledge like it's going out of style."[45]

Because Tiger lived in California and he was in Houston, Texas, Harmon mainly coached him by telephone. Tiger also sent Harmon a videotape each month so his coach could analyze his swing.

Playing—and Losing—Against the Pros

Fifteen-year-old Tiger first met Jack Nicklaus in April 1991 when his idol gave a clinic at Bel Air Country Club in West Los Angeles. After he watched Tiger swing a few times, Nicklaus said admiringly, "When I grow up I want to have a swing as pretty as yours."[46] It was a swing that had been honed by members of Team Tiger.

The same year he met Nicklaus, Tiger took that wonderful swing and played in a qualifying tournament for a spot in the Los Angeles Open, a PGA tour event. He failed to win a berth in the field by just three strokes but in 1992 the Los Angeles Open granted him a sponsor's exemption and that February, at the age of sixteen years and two months, Tiger became the youngest golfer ever to play in a professional tournament.

Now grown to his full height of six feet, two inches but still a skinny 140 pounds, Tiger shot a respectable one over par 72 in his first round. His first shot on the Riviera Country Club course in Pacific Palisades, California, was a 280-yard drive with a three wood. He hit the green with another three wood and birdied the par-5, 501-yard hole despite being nervous. "I was so tense," he said, "I had a tough time holding the club. It was like rigor mortis had set in." [47]

Huge galleries followed Tiger around the course, shouting out supportive phrases like "You the kid!," a variation of the mantra "You the man!" many fans shout at their favorite golfers. But Tiger stumbled to a 75 the next day and missed the cut, which meant he could not play in the final two rounds.

Tiger Woods nervously watches his ball after stroking a putt in the 1993 Los Angeles Open.

One of Tiger's strengths is his ability to look at himself objectively, something many athletes fail to do, especially when they are successful at a young age. Now, Tiger was able to realize he was still not ready to compete on equal terms with the pros. "I'm not mature enough," he admitted. "My body hasn't finished growing and my swing's not good enough. It's not fine-tuned. The guys on the pro tour don't make dumb decisions. Their thinking is very clear. With me, sixteen-year-old problems sneak in there every once in a while. I still take too many chances, get too emotional and try things that aren't very smart." [48]

In 1993, at age seventeen, Tiger received exemptions to play in the Los Angeles Open, Honda Classic, and Byron Nelson Classic. He was still struggling against the pros but his golfing ability, considered a freak of nature when he was swinging away while still in diapers, had quickly matured because of Team Tiger.

Tiger Goes to College

Every college with a major golf program offered Tiger a scholarship, but he chose Stanford University because of its high academic standards. He entered Stanford in the fall of 1994,
majoring in business because he wanted to learn how to handle
the large sums of money he expected to make when he turned
professional. In his first semester, his classes included mathe-
matics, civics, and computer technology.

Tiger quickly became the star on a team Coach Wally
Goodwin had guided the previous year to the National
Collegiate Athletic Association (NCAA) title. Tiger won his first
college tournament, the Tucker Invitational at the University of
New Mexico, by three strokes and by the middle of the season
was the nation's top-ranked college player.

He found not only golf success at Stanford but a place where
he could fit in despite his precocious golfing ability and growing
fame. Other students, Tiger discovered, had talents as great as
his own. "It's so challenging," he said. "I thought one of the guys
in my dorm was a big, dumb, stereotypical football player, a six-
foot-six lineman. He scored fifteen hundred on his SATs. You get
guys talking like that intelligently to you, it's pretty shocking.
Another guy who scored 1508 on his SATs never studies because
he has a photographic memory. It's great. But it's weird. When
I was in high school, I set the curve. Here I follow it."[49]

His Stanford teammates included Notah Begay, a Native
American; Will Yanigasawa, a Chinese American; and Casey
Martin, who would become well known himself in 1997 for his successful lawsuit forcing the PGA to allow him to use a cart in competition. Martin suffers from a disease that has shriveled the muscles in
his right leg and makes it difficult for him to walk a golf course.

Despite his celebrity and success, Woods was just one of the
guys on the golf team. Begay, a close friend since their days in
junior golf, nicknamed him Urkel, after the character on the television sitcom *Family Matters,* because Woods sports thick glasses
when he does not wear his contact lenses. Tiger didn't like the
nickname—he already had one of the greatest in sports—but he
put up with the good-natured razzing.

Tiger Is Robbed

Although Tiger Woods enjoyed attending Stanford University, a frightening incident occurred his first year when he was mugged late at night in a campus parking lot.

Tiger was returning to his dormitory room from a charity dinner in San Francisco when a robber attacked him. The man held a knife to his throat; after taking a watch and gold chain, he punched Tiger in the face with the handle of the knife, knocking Tiger to the ground. Tiger did not have his wallet and the attacker might have been angry that his victim did not have any money he could steal. The scariest thing was that the robber knew who Tiger was, calling him by name as he struck him.

Just a few hours later, however, Tiger was able to joke about the incident when he called his dad. "I talked to him at 2 A.M.," Woods remembers. "He said, 'Pops, you know that overbite I had? It's gone. My teeth are all perfectly aligned.'" Tiger reported the incident to campus police, who never found his assailant.

When he returned home after the incident, his mother took him to a Buddhist temple to be blessed for good luck in the future. Also, sports psychologist Jay Brunza counseled Tiger so he would not have any bad emotional aftereffects from the incident.

The negative side of fame and celebrity is that the famous sometimes become targets. The person who robbed Tiger knew who he was and may have thought he would be carrying a lot of money.

Tiger Woods lines up a putt in June 1996 in the NCAA Men's Championship at the Honor's Course in Ooltewah, Tennessee. He added the NCAA men's title that year to his impressive list of amateur victories.

The U.S. Amateur Championship

Though he won the NCAA individual title in 1996, Tiger did not have a brilliant college career in his two seasons of competition. It seemed he was more excited about playing in professional tournaments, including one in his mother's native Thailand when he was a freshman in 1994 and his first Masters in 1995, and competing in the U.S. Amateur Championship and other top amateur tournaments.

The Amateur is a grueling test that begins with two rounds of medal play; the sixty-four players shooting the lowest scores advance to six rounds of match play. Winning this prestigious event was more important to Tiger than any college event could ever be, and his record three straight victories from 1994 to 1996 may well define him as the greatest amateur golfer of all time.

A few weeks before entering Stanford, Tiger won his first Amateur in dramatic fashion by overcoming a huge deficit at the Tournament Players Club–Sawgrass Stadium course in Ponte

Vedra, Florida. In the thirty-six-hole finale against Trip Kuehne, a twenty-two-year-old junior at Oklahoma State, Tiger struggled early and trailed by four holes after the first eighteen holes.

Earl Woods, however, never wavered in his belief his son would win. "Let the legend grow," he told Tiger at the lunch break between rounds.[50] He was telling Tiger that he knew he had the ability to pull off yet another stunning comeback. When the deficit grew even larger, reaching six after thirteen holes,

Tiger's First U.S. Amateur Championship

The dramatic way Tiger Woods has won many tournaments has added to his mystique. A case in point is his first U.S. Amateur title in September 1994 when he once again had to battle from behind to win.

Tim Rosaforte, who wrote about the tournament in the September 5 issue of *Sports Illustrated*, said the key shot came on the seventeenth hole, the famous island green at the Tournament Players Club–Sawgrass Stadium course in Ponte Vedra, Florida. Playing it for the second time that day, Woods boldly went for the pin—a move that could have resulted in his ball's going in the water because of the hole's location. This is how Rosaforte described the shot.

"On the 17th tee Tiger Woods never gave a second thought to the water surrounding the hole's infamous island green. In his hands he first held a nine-iron, then exchanged it in favor of a pitching wedge with lead tape on the back. He had 139 yards to the stick, the wind at his back and the heart of a young lion thumping in his chest. His target? 'The pin,' he would say later. 'I was going directly at the pin.' This was the defining moment for Woods in a U.S. Amateur comeback victory that bordered on the impossible: six down after 13 holes of the 36-hole match play final, five down with 12 holes remaining, three down going to the final nine.

Woods's fearless tee shot landed in a nearly impossible place—to the right of the flag, positioned far to the green's right side. The ball first hit just four paces from the water's edge. Woods's mother, Kultida, watching on TV at home in Cypress, California, [said], 'That boy almost gave me a heart attack. All I kept saying was, "God, don't let that ball go in the water." That boy tried to kill me.'

The ball spun into the fringe, took a soft bounce in the rough and spun back onto the collar just past pin high and no more than three feet from the water. The ensuing putt [of fourteen feet] dropped for a birdie. [The birdie putt gave him a one-up lead over Trip Kuehne and a closing par on the final hole gave him the title.]"

things looked bleak, but Tiger kept his composure, played steady golf, and narrowed the deficit to three holes going into the final nine.

Tiger then mounted his final electrifying charge, winning the tenth, eleventh, sixteenth, seventeenth, and eighteenth holes.

He tied the match by winning the sixteenth hole but the most dramatic shot came at the seventeenth, the course's famous island hole, when Tiger ignored the threat of water to fire directly at the pin. His ball, after spinning back dangerously close to the edge of the water, landed fourteen feet from the hole. He calmly sank the birdie putt to finally take the lead and

In August 1996 Tiger Woods kisses his historic third U.S. Amateur championship trophy, which he won at Pumpkin Ridge near Portland, Oregon.

when the ball dropped, Tiger pumped his right arm in the fierce uppercut that has become his trademark signature of triumph. The two golfers halved the final hole with pars, giving Tiger the victory.

"It's an amazing feeling to come from that many down to beat a great player. It's indescribable,"[51] said Tiger, who had overcome the biggest deficit in the history of the tournament to win.

Tiger was the youngest and first black amateur champion in the event as well as the first golfer to win both the U.S. Junior and U.S. Amateur titles. "When Tiger won his first U.S. Junior . . . I said to him, 'Son, you have done something no black person in the United States has ever done, and you will forever be part of history.' But this is ungodly in its ramifications,"[52] his father said.

Tiger was ecstatic not only because he had won but because the victory gave him automatic berths in the Masters and British Open the following year. He would finally play in a major event with the best players in the world.

Chapter 4

The Greatest Amateur Ever Turns Pro

O<small>NE OF THE</small> articles in the December 26, 1994, edition of *Newsweek* magazine carried the headline "Great Names, Great Games." The story claimed Tiger Woods and Venus Williams, a fourteen-year-old tennis sensation who had already turned professional, represented "the next generation of superstar athletes, youngsters graced with the skills, the grins—and the memorable first names—to play right through the millennium."[53]

Tiger was hailed as "golf's child champ, at 18 the youngest winner ever of the U.S. Amateur. He is a new hero, emerging just as the baby boom starts picking up golf sticks." After listing his many accomplishments, it ended, "And he's only just begun."[54]

The article's subtitle was "Phenoms Venus Williams and Tiger Woods will shake up the country clubs." The reason is that both were black athletes excelling in sports that were traditionally played by affluent whites at country clubs, some of which still barred black members.

Just a few months later, Tiger fulfilled that second prophecy about shaking up the mostly white country club set by playing in the Masters.

Tiger's First Masters

For many golfing fans, Augusta National Golf Club and the Masters symbolize all that is wonderful about golf. One of the world's most beautiful and challenging courses, Augusta National is rich in the history of the game not only because of the tournament it hosts each year but because it was cofounded by Bobby Jones, the golfer who until Tiger was considered the greatest amateur of all time.

But to some the course in Augusta, Georgia, is also a symbol of the racist attitudes that have often excluded blacks from golf. When Tiger drove down Magnolia Lane to enter Augusta National in April 1995, he was one of the few blacks to ever do so to play golf. Augusta National had barred black members for most of its history, with cofounder Clifford Roberts once defiantly proclaiming, "As long as I'm alive, golfers will be white, and caddies will be black."[55] Augusta National did not accept its first black member until 1991, after the PGA ruled that clubs that restricted their membership to whites could not host tournaments.

The Masters is a privately run tournament in which participants are invited; no black received an invitation until 1975, when Lee Elder finally broke the color barrier. Because Tiger was only the fourth black to play in the tournament's sixty-one year history and the first considered good enough to win, his debut became a major event. *Newsweek* magazine stated: "When [Tiger] tees off in the first round of the Masters at Augusta, Ga., this Thursday as the most acclaimed teenage player in history—having surpassed the amateur records of both Bobby Jones and Jack Nicklaus—his blissfully sweet swing, mature countenance, and sheer outrageous ability will confirm the arrival, finally, of golf's first black superstar."[56]

In 1975 Lee Elder became the first black to play in the Masters. Other great black golfers had deserved to play in the tournament years before Elder but were never invited because of the racist attitude of the private club.

Tiger lived up to that advance billing though his nerves betrayed him on the first hole. After a long drive and a second shot that found the green, Tiger had a thirty-foot birdie putt. The greens at Augusta National are notoriously fast. Tiger had tried to prepare by practicing on Stanford's basketball floor but his first putt rolled past the cup, off the green, and wound up fifty feet from the hole. "I lost my focus on that putt," Tiger admits. "I went brain dead." [57]

After that opening bogey 5, he got his nerves under control. Tiger birdied the next hole and finished with an even par 72, four shots better than the scores of Jack Nicklaus and Arnold Palmer in their Masters' debuts, and another 72 Friday helped him make the thirty-six-hole cut so he could play the final two rounds. Tiger ballooned to a third round 77 but a solid 72 Sunday gave him a five over par total of 293, the lowest for all amateurs and forty-first overall. He finished just fifteen shots behind winner Ben Crenshaw and led the field in driving, averaging just over 311 yards.

The "Crow's Nest"

"To tell you the truth," Tiger said, "I had the time of my life." [58] The teen sensation spent an entire week at Augusta National playing practice rounds with stars like Greg Norman and Nick Faldo; sleeping in the "Crow's Nest," rooms traditionally set aside for amateurs; answering questions almost daily from the assembled news media, whose members eagerly told his story to the world; and drawing huge numbers of fans wherever he went.

Before Tiger left Augusta, he delivered a note to tournament officials thanking them for his wonderful experience:

> I was treated like a gentleman throughout my stay and I trust I responded in kind. The "Crow's Nest" will always remain in my heart and your magnificent golf course will provide a continuing challenge throughout my amateur and professional career. I've accomplished much here and learned even more. Your tournament will always hold a special place in my heart as the place where I made my first PGA cut and at a major yet! It is here that I left my youth and became a man. For that I will be

eternally in your debt. With warmest regards and deepest appreciation, I remain, sincerely, Tiger Woods.[59]

Although disappointed with his play after the third round, Tiger had gestured at photographs of past champions and made a prophecy to reporters: "Someday," he said with a smile, "I'm going to get my picture up there."[60]

Tiger and Racism

Many people who watched Tiger on television sent him letters in care of Augusta National. One type of mail he had grown accustomed to receiving was racist hate mail. "Just what we need," one letter said, "another nigger in sports."[61]

Tiger had been a target of racists ever since that day in 1981 when he was tied to a tree and taunted for being black on his first day in kindergarten. In 1992, when he played his first round in the Los Angeles Open at age sixteen, Riviera Country Club received several telephone death threats aimed at Tiger by people upset that a black man had received an exemption. Two

Wearing a Stanford baseball cap, Tiger Woods hits a drive in the 1995 Masters. His sensational debut marked a major step forward in his career.

years later in a U.S. Amateur match against Buddy Alexander, the golf coach at the University of Florida, a female spectator was overheard saying, "Who do you think those people are rooting for, the nigger or the Gator coach."[62]

The volume of threats and hate mail increased as Tiger became more famous. Instead of ignoring racism, Tiger confronted it, reading hate mail and taping some letters to the wall of his Stanford dormitory room. "Tiger has always received hate mail, which he reads," his father says. "And I approve of that; I don't want him to be surprised. I want him to know."[63]

While Tiger was growing up, Earl Woods educated his son about the struggles black golfers had overcome to win the right to play professionally. The PGA had enforced a Caucasians-only policy until 1961, just fourteen years before Tiger was born, robbing talented black golfers of the chance to prove themselves against top white golfers. "I've taught that young man black history," his father says, "so that he can know and appreciate those who came before him and made it possible for him to walk down that fairway."[64]

After the second round of the Masters, the father and son further acknowledged that debt by staging a golf clinic at nearby Forest Hills, a course where blacks played. "It's a black thing," says Earl. "We realize the debt [Tiger owes to black golfers of the past]. It's a way of saying thank you and a promise to carry the baton."[65]

Woods says he and his son share an awareness of how whites sometimes react when they encounter blacks in normally all-white domains:

> He knows all about "The Look." We used to go into the country clubs, and "The Look" says: "What the hell are you doing here?" I can remember going with Tiger to an all-male country club outside of Chicago, when he was the current U.S. Junior champion. And as soon as we stepped in there, the conversation stopped, like somebody had yanked down the venetian blinds. Everything stopped and did not resume until we sat down. And then it buzzed. Tiger said to me, "You feel it, dad?" I said, "Of course, I feel it."[66]

Tiger understands how racism has tainted golf's past but realizes that the sport is changing, partly due to his own impact.

"Golf was originated in Scotland by rich whites," Tiger has said. "When it was brought over here, we made our country clubs exclusively for whites. Minorities, they just served as cooks, porters, and caddies. So it's refreshing to see some changes happening."[67]

Tiger Wins Another Amateur

Although a few people have had trouble accepting a black golf star, many people, black and white, were happy a black had finally become one of the biggest names in the game. They were intrigued with the story of his life, his dramatic flair on the golf course, and his engaging personality.

For the most part, his new fans had little to cheer about in 1995 as Tiger failed to live up to his splendid Masters debut. Bothered by several nagging ailments, including a wrist injury that forced him to withdraw after five holes in the second round of the U.S. Open, Tiger struggled with his game. He tied for sixty-seventh in the British Open and played in several other professional events, but he won just one college tournament, the Stanford Invitational, and only tied for fifth in the NCAA Championship. The media quickly began questioning whether Tiger was overrated or if the tall, skinny golfer was too frail to stand up to the demands of the game.

But Tiger answered his critics by winning a second straight U.S. Amateur championship, a feat Jack Nicklaus never accomplished. Tiger never trailed in match play at the Newport (Rhode Island) Country Club until his thirty-six-hole finale against George "Buddy" Marucci Jr., a forty-three-year-old import car dealer from Berwyn, Pennsylvania. His older opponent had a surprising three-hole lead after twelve holes but Tiger came back to lead by two holes with two to play and only had to tie Marucci on the final hole to become the ninth person to win two straight titles.

Both players had good drives on the last hole and Marucci, hitting first from the fairway, landed his second shot just twenty feet from the hole. The pressure was now on Tiger to get his shot close. From 140 yards, Woods hit the key shot of the tournament—a soft eight iron that placed the ball just inches from the hole. After Marucci missed his birdie attempt and made par, he graciously conceded Tiger's birdie putt, giving him the match.

Tiger Woods smashes a long drive during a practice round for the 1995 Masters while playing partners Ray Floyd (left) and Greg Norman (center) watch.

The eight-iron shot was a new weapon in Tiger's golf arsenal, something he and coach Claude "Butch" Harmon had been working on since the Masters. Harmon wanted Tiger to learn how to hit shots at half-strength when yardage dictated it. This was not easy for Tiger, who liked to swing as hard as possible with every club, but he had finally mastered the new technique.

"That's something he couldn't have done at Augusta," said Harmon. "Last spring, he would have hit pitching wedge as hard as he could, and it would have sucked back off the green. But, on that last swing, he went down the shaft on an eight-iron and hit it stiff. The fact that he attempted it on the last shot of the tournament is why I'm so proud of him. That was the beauty of all the work we've done."[68]

To Go Pro Or Not To Go Pro?

Tiger dedicated himself in the off season to gaining strength, adding fifteen pounds of muscle through lifting weights and good nutrition, and by the time he returned to the Masters in April of 1996 he was

Tiger and the NCAA

The National Collegiate Athletic Association (NCAA) is the governing body for college sports. The NCAA issues and enforces regulations to protect the amateur status of athletes, including rules that limit money or gifts they can receive. For Tiger Woods, NCAA rules were often a source of irritation.

In April 1995 after returning to Stanford from the Masters, the school suspended Tiger Woods from the golf team for a day for a possible rules violation: He had written diaries for *Golf World* and *Golfweek* magazines on his Masters debut. The school was also concerned because Tiger used new irons in the final round that belonged to Claude "Butch" Harmon Jr. and accepted some golf balls from Greg Norman. NCAA rules say players can use only equipment provided by their schools.

In October of that year, Tiger had dinner with Arnold Palmer at the Silverado Country Club in Napa, California. Tiger offered to pay but Palmer, one of the greatest golfers of all time and a millionaire many times over, picked up the check. Tiger told his coach, Wally Goodwin, about the meal. The result of Tiger's honesty was that he was again declared ineligible until he wrote Palmer a check for $25 to cover his share of the dinner because NCAA rules do not allow athletes to accept such gratuities.

Woods biographer Tim Rosaforte said the incident upset Tiger and helped push him toward turning pro. "I was pretty angry," Tiger said."I felt like I didn't do anything wrong by having dinner and talking about things I wanted to talk about. I was declared ineligible. It's annoying."

The rules mishap had a happy ending when Goodwin asked Tiger for the canceled check. He auctioned it for $2,500 at a dinner to raise funds to send area youths to a Stanford golf camp for junior players.

outdriving Greg Norman, one of the game's longest hitters, by fifty and sixty yards. But his second Masters was disappointing and Tiger missed the cut after two straight three over par 75s.

The rest of the year, however, Tiger was nearly invincible as he won nine of thirteen college tournaments, including the NCAA Championship, and led Stanford to the PAC-10 title. Tiger also began to prove he was ready for the PGA tour as he made the cut in the U.S. Open, finishing tied for eighty-second, and had a stellar performance at the British Open at Royal Lytham and St. Annes in England. His seventy-two-hole total of 281 tied the record for an amateur in the prestigious event and his five-under-par 66 in the second round was the lowest by an amateur since Frank Stranahan in 1950.

Speculation had grown since his first Masters that Tiger would soon turn professional, but when to take that important step in his life was a difficult decision. Tiger, who knew his parents valued education, had vowed to finish college but the lure of millions of dollars, his growing boredom playing against overmatched amateurs, his desire to test himself full-time against the world's best golfers, and a series of minor but irritating encounters with NCAA officials over rules governing athletes all helped change his mind. His brilliant 66 in the British Open was also a factor in his decision.

"Something really clicked that day," he said, "like I had found a whole new style of playing. I finally understood the meaning of playing within myself." [69] Tiger began to ask golfers like Norman, Nicklaus, and Ernie Els about whether he should turn pro: They all told him he was ready. "I just said, 'You're good enough to play out here,'" said Els.[70]

But Tiger had one final amateur goal: to be the first golfer to win three U.S. Amateur championships. The tournament was

Greg Norman and Tiger Woods share a lighter moment as they stroll down the fairway during the 1996 Masters.

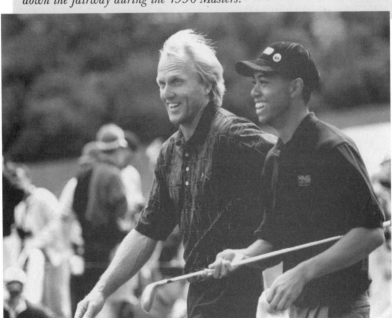

held in late August at the Pumpkin Ridge golf complex near Portland, Oregon. Tiger opened the tournament with a 67 and 69 to win medalist honors and easily advanced through match play to the title round against Steve Scott of the University of Florida. Scott played brilliantly, going four up after the first eighteen holes and leading by five with sixteen left.

Tiger found himself in the same situation as in 1994 when he was so far behind that it looked like he could not win. It was simply time for another dramatic comeback. Beginning on the twenty-first hole Tiger won three straight holes and he tied Scott on the thirty-fifth with a magnificent thirty-five-foot birdie putt. When the ball dropped into the hole, Tiger celebrated with a jubilant uppercut in the air. After halving the thirty-sixth and final hole the two young golfers went to sudden death, with Woods winning on the second hole with a par 3.

Tiger had emerged victorious in his last amateur event. He was now ready to fulfill his destiny by joining the ranks of the world's professional golfers.

Tiger Turns Pro at the GMO

With four simple words, Tiger Woods left the ranks of amateur golf: "I guess, hello, world."[71] Three days after wrapping up his historic U.S. Amateur triple, Tiger Woods used those words on August 28 to begin his news conference at the Greater Milwaukee Open (GMO), the tournament in which he would make his professional debut the next day. "It wasn't about money," Tiger said. "It was about happiness. The time was right. I knew my golf game was good enough. It boiled down to how happy am I? And I'm happy."[72]

Tiger was also rich. In the few days between the U.S. Amateur and the GMO, International Management Group (IMG) had worked out details for endorsement contracts with Nike and Titleist, two large, well-known companies that make sportswear and golf equipment, that were worth an estimated $60 million over five years. IMG, the most powerful sports marketing company in the world, names among its clients Muhammad Ali, Wayne Gretzky, Joe Montana, Nancy Lopez, and Arnold Palmer.

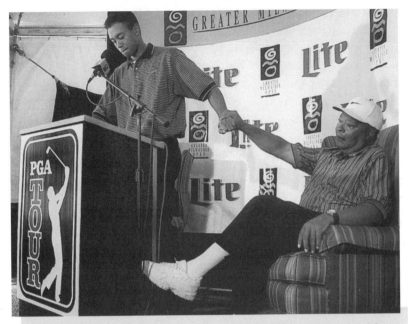

Tiger Woods reassuringly clasps hands with his father, Earl, during the news conference in which he announces his decision to become a professional golfer.

The Nike deal included a $7.5 million signing bonus, but Tiger was still only a paper millionaire while IMG was negotiating the final details of the lucrative agreements. "I haven't signed for any money yet. I haven't seen a penny yet. I haven't seen any check in the mail yet. I'm still broke,"[73] he told reporters. In fact, on the way to Brown Deer Park golf course Tiger had to borrow from Harmon to pay the $100 GMO entrance fee. And the night before, at dinner, all Tiger had in his pockets was $25 worth of McDonald's gift certificates.

However, at the GMO Tiger did begin enjoying some of the perks of his newfound pro status. He was excited that tournament officials lent him a car to drive—"I still can't rent a car, but they gave me a courtesy car"—and that Nike had sent him a new golf wardrobe. "I got all these clothes delivered Wednesday," he excitedly told reporters. "The best thing was they came in these great bags. They're unbelievable bags. They have all these unbelievable pockets and stuff. Just the best."[74]

Tiger will never have an empty wallet again, but he was more concerned about the total on his scorecard at the end of the GMO than his bank balance. "In my life, I've never gone to a tournament thinking I couldn't win," Woods said. "That's just my mind-set. It's something I've always believed in. It's something I always will."[75]

Tiger, however, found out it was harder beating pro golfers than amateurs. The first hole he played was a 450-yard par 4; he delighted the huge gallery by booming his first drive 336 yards down the middle of the fairway. He shot a first round four under par 67, a score good enough to lead almost any amateur field, but was five shots behind leader Nolan Henke.

"Fluff" Cowan

Tiger tied for sixtieth in his first tournament; except for a hole-in-one on the 202-yard par-3 fourteenth hole in the final round, he played solidly but not spectacularly. But it had been a difficult week, one in which he won his third U.S. Amateur, made his final decision to turn pro, consulted on deals with IMG, hired veteran caddie Michael "Fluff" Cowan, and dealt with more reporters than some athletes meet in a lifetime.

Caddie Mike "Fluff" Cowan helps Tiger Woods line up a putt. The veteran caddie helped Tiger adjust to life on the pro tour and quickly became a friend to the young golfer.

"Overall, it was a lot of fun," Woods said of his first tournament, which included a final round 68. "I was able to play pretty good, coming off a big week."[76] The lackluster start in his pro career had not mattered to hordes of fans who turned out to witness golf history. The GMO, a tournament that rarely attracts the top stars, benefited from the Tiger factor to set

The PGA's Odd Couple: "Tiger" and "Fluff"

On the surface, Tiger Woods and Michael "Fluff" Cowan appear to be the oddest couple on the PGA tour, the tall, slender, dynamic golf superstar and his short, dumpy, white-haired caddy, whose walrus-style mustache adorns a weatherbeaten face that bears testimony to the rigors of more than twenty years of toting bags for professional golfers.

But for all their differences, they make a great team. "I think Fluff's the best caddy in the world. He's a great caddy and a great friend," Woods said in *Sports Illustrated*.

When Tiger turned pro, he needed an experienced caddy, one familiar with the courses he would now play as well as the day-to-day details of life on the tour. He chose Fluff, who had caddied the last nineteen years for Peter Jacobsen but who in the summer of 1996 was out of a job because Jacobsen hurt his back. When Tiger called him after winning his last amateur title, it was an opportunity of a lifetime for Fluff even though he hated leaving Jacobsen, a close friend. "I never made this change for money," said Fluff. "I was doing fine for money. Peter treated me like a king. I made it [to watch golf] history. And now I've got the best seat in the house."

Caddies do more than carry bags and wash dirty balls. They advise golfers on yardage and club selection, calm them down when they hit bad shots, and help in many other ways. In the final round of the 1997 Pebble Beach National Pro-Am, Tiger wanted to hit a six iron into the par-3 seventeenth hole. Fluff advised a seven iron. "So I changed and I hit it to about three feet and made birdie," said Tiger. "He's a pretty mellow guy and it helps to have a guy who's mellow and yet who can speak up and say his opinion when he has to."

And Fluff appreciates working with perhaps the greatest golfer ever. "I'm just enjoying the ride," he says.

an attendance record of 150,000. Kultida Woods, who attended the tournament with Earl, was overcome by the huge numbers of fans who followed her son. "It was like he was the pope,"[77] she said.

At the news conference in which Tiger announced he was turning pro, Earl had told reporters: "He's like an Old West gunslinger, like the fastest gun in the West."[78] Before long Tiger could begin carving notches in his gun belt symbolizing his first professional victories.

Chapter 5

A True Master of Golf

THE OCTOBER 28, 1996, cover of *Sports Illustrated* featured Tiger Woods and the startling headline "Tiger! In two months as a pro, he has transformed an entire sport." The cover of the November issue of *Golf Digest* asked, "Is This Kid Superman?"

After his humble start at the Greater Milwaukee Open, Tiger finished eleventh in the Canadian Open, fifth at the Quad City Classic, and third in the British Columbia Open. In just four weeks Tiger had made more than $140,000, enough to finish among the top 125 money winners for the year; enough to earn a spot on the Professional Golfers Association tour in 1997, a daunting task many had believed was beyond Tiger in the few tournaments he would play.

But those heroics were just a prelude to the Las Vegas Invitational, a ninety-hole tournament held October 2 through October 6. After a mediocre opening score of 70 left him trailing the leaders by eight strokes, Tiger roared back with a 63, 68, 67, and a final round 64 to tie Davis Love III. On the first playoff hole Love, one of the best players in the world, and Tiger both belted long drives, but Tiger put his second shot eighteen feet from the hole while Love hit into a sand trap. Love made a bogey 5 while Tiger two-putted for his first professional victory.

"Yeah, I kind of did," Tiger said unemotionally when asked if he believed he could win so soon. "I don't see any of this as scary or a burden. I've always known where I wanted to go in life. I've never let anything deter me. This is my purpose. *It will unfold.*"[79]

Tiger simply knew he was fulfilling the destiny his father set for him when he began teaching him golf as an infant. Two weeks later Tiger won the Walt Disney World/Oldsmobile Classic in his new hometown of Orlando, Florida. He had amassed nearly $750,000 in seven weeks, climbed to twenty-third on the PGA money list, and qualified for the season-ending Tour Championship.

"Oh, god," moaned tour veteran Peter Jacobsen after Tiger's second victory. "If this is how he is every week, then it's over. He's the greatest player in the history of the game."[80]

Tigermania

In the October 28 *Sports Illustrated* cover story, author Rick Reilly wrote that Tiger had not only transformed the competitive landscape of golf but the makeup of fans who attended tournaments: "To understand what golf is now, don't watch Tiger Woods. Watch who *watches* Tiger Woods." Reilly noted that Tiger was luring a new breed of fan to golf tournaments, including young black women and Hispanic teens visiting a golf course for the very first time, "giant groups of fourth-graders, mimicking their first golf swings," and "mothers with strollers catching the wheels in the bunkers as they go."[81]

In seven weeks Tiger lured an extra 150,000 people to events like the GMO and Quad Cities Classic, tournaments that normally did not draw well. Television ratings were also higher than ever as millions tuned in to see this new superstar. Many of those fans, both at the golf course and at home, had cared nothing for golf until Tiger came along.

Tiger's smiling face now became a common sight on magazine covers, even mainstream publications, like *Business Week,* that had never before featured golf. Nike and Titleist saturated the airwaves with Tiger commercials and sites devoted to him began popping up on the Internet.

Tigermania had begun. It would come into full bloom in April at the Masters.

Masters Champion

Tiger began 1997 hotter than ever by winning the season-opening Mercedes Championships, beating Tom Lehman in a

*Tiger Woods with his mom, Kultida, after winning the Asian Honda
Classic in Thailand.*

playoff with a birdie on the par-3 seventh hole. His spectacular
six-iron shot drew perfectly to the flag, landed two feet to the
right of the hole, and spun back to within inches to give him the
victory. In a sentimental journey home with his mother, Tiger
next won the Asian Honda Classic in Thailand in mid-February
by ten strokes. Tida and her son were treated as royalty and
Prime Minister General Chavalit Yongchaiyudh granted Tiger
honorary Thai citizenship.

In April, Tiger went to Augusta the clear favorite to win one
of golf's most coveted prizes. But with the eyes of the world
upon him, Tiger stumbled over the first nine holes to a four-
over-par 40. Suddenly, Tiger looked all too human.

But then, as had happened so often in the past, something
magical occurred. While trudging to the tenth tee, Tiger realized
what he was doing wrong—his backswing was way too long, resulting in errant shots. When he corrected that flaw by shorten-
ing his swing, he birdied the tenth, twelfth, and thirteenth holes,
eagled the fifteenth and finished the last two holes with a birdie

and a par for a blazing six-under-par 30. His two-under 70 placed him just three shots back of leader John Huston.

Tiger shot a blistering 66 on Friday to take a three-shot lead and Saturday increased his lead to nine by shooting 65. The final round on Sunday was to be nothing more than a victory march for Tiger, who would become the youngest golfer—twenty-one years, three months, fourteen days—and the first black to win the Masters. That Saturday night he had a long talk with his dad, who was at the tournament despite having had heart bypass surgery just two months earlier. "Last night my pop and I were talking," Woods said. "He said, 'Son, this will be probably one of the hardest rounds you've ever had to play in your life. And if you just go out there and be yourself, it will be one of the most rewarding rounds of golf you ever played in your life.'"[82]

His round was that and more, perhaps the most memorable ever played in a major tournament. Despite carrying the weight of history on his broad shoulders, Woods, clad in a red shirt, the color his mom urges him to wear for luck on Sundays, shot 69. He not only won the title by an unbelievable dozen shots but demolished sacred Augusta National with a record total eighteen-under-par 270. It was just one of more than a half-dozen Masters records he set.

On the eighteenth tee a camera clicked twice on his backswing, causing him to hook his drive left. Tiger hit a wedge shot to the green but after missing a birdie putt, he needed to

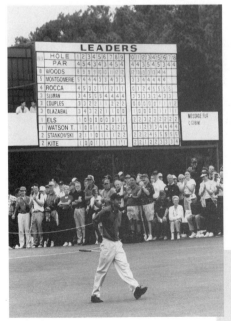

Tiger Woods strides confidently onto the 17th green at Augusta National during the third round of the 1997 Masters.

sink a tricky five footer for par to beat the record of 271 Jack Nicklaus set in 1965.

When the putt dropped, Tiger hugged his caddy, Michael "Fluff" Cowan, and then sought out his dad. "We did it, Pop! We did it!"[83] Tiger said as they embraced. He then embraced his mother and afterward, as he made his way through the cheering crowd to be interviewed on television, Tiger spotted Charlie Sifford. Another hug ensued and Tiger told the pioneering black golfer, "Thanks for making this possible."[84] The tribute left Sifford in tears.

The fact that his Masters victory came exactly fifty years after Jackie Robinson became the first black to break the color line

Tiger's Power

In golf, no one is more revered than the player who can hit the ball the farthest. A long drive not only looks dramatic, it makes the rest of the hole easier to play. How long is Tiger Woods? So long that he amazes even his fellow professionals, most of whom can routinely drive the ball 280 yards or more themselves.

A *Sports Illustrated* story that appeared several weeks after he turned pro included this exchange between two golfers about how far Tiger can hit the ball.

"Man, you should have seen how Tiger was hitting," Paul Goydos said to John Cook after having to play directly behind Woods in the Walt Disney World/Oldsmobile Classic. "You'd have been humbled." "C'mon." said Cook. "What's so humbling?" "How 'bout he reaches number 8 [614 yards] in two [shots]?" Silence. "Now *that*," said Cook, "is humbling."

While average golfers are ecstatic to hit their drives 200 yards, Woods can hit it twice that far. At a tournament in 1998 at Castle Pines Golf Course in Castle Rock, Colorado, he hit a drive 403 yards. Even considering that a ball travels farther at higher altitudes, it was an unbelievable shot.

Tiger began developing his reputation for power early. When Tiger was just sixteen years old he played a round of golf in Florida with Greg Norman, who is known for his own ability to hit long drives. "That little whippersnapper was driving it by me," Norman said.

Although Tiger is not big physically, he is very strong from lifting weights and is very flexible. The key to hitting the ball long is generating clubhead speed, and Tiger is able to use his strength, balance, and finely tuned swing to drive the ball farther and straighter than nearly anyone else ever has.

by playing major league baseball did not escape the new champion's attention. "Obviously, Jackie Robinson is one of my heroes," he said:

> He has definitely inspired me. All the people who were against him doing something he loved to do was unfortunately a sign of the times. But if it wasn't for him, I don't know if other players such as Lee Elder or even Charlie [Sifford] could have done the things they did. . . . Jackie was the one who paved the way for all pioneers who are minorities.[85]

A Corporate Tiger

Tiger won the Byron Nelson Classic in his next start and the Western Open in July. He was ranked number one in the world on July 15, reaching the top spot faster (forty-two weeks) and at a younger age than any golfer before him. It had taken Germany's Bernhard Langer, who was twenty-nine when he reached the top spot in the Sony rankings in 1986, 177 weeks to become number one.

But when Tiger's game seemed to decline after winning the Western and he failed to challenge in the three remaining majors in 1997—the U.S. Open, British Open, and PGA Championship—speculation began to build that his new lifestyle was to blame. One factor may have been the huge amount of time he now had to devote to his growing business interests.

By the time Tiger walked off the eighteenth green at Augusta, he had become one of the richest athletes in the world. In addition to a green sports jacket, Tiger collected $486,000 for his historic victory at Augusta. The $216,000 he pocketed in January for winning the Mercedes tournament had already pushed his career earnings to $1 million as he reached that magical mark in fewer tournaments than any player in PGA history (nine) and, naturally, became the youngest to do so at twenty-one years and fourteen days.

But the money Tiger made playing golf was small change compared to the tens of millions of dollars he was receiving in endorsements from Nike, Titleist, and other companies. An article titled "Tiger, Inc." in the April 28 issue of *Business Week* asked:

British golf star Nick Faldo helps Tiger Woods don the traditional green jacket given to the tournament's champion.

Has any athlete, anywhere, anytime come this far this fast? In the space of a little more than seven months, Eldrick "Tiger" Woods has become a sports legend whose name is spoken in the same breath as Babe Ruth, Jackie Robinson, Pele, Muhammad Ali, and Michael Jordan. At 21, he has turned the whitebread world of golf on its ear, captured the imagination of millions who know nothing about the game, and positioned himself as arguably the most sought-after pitchman in America.[86]

On the day he turned pro, Tiger became an instant millionaire with his five-year endorsement deals for Nike (an estimated $40 million) and Titleist (an estimated $20 million). But International Management Group (IMG), realizing the young golfer would be a valuable commodity for many years, decided to go slow on other commitments. Tiger later signed to represent Rolex watches and American Express credit cards, and became one of the celebrity partners in the All-Star Cafe restaurant franchise, but in early 1998

IMG founder Mark McCormack said he did not want his star client to become burned out by business.

"He's got to concentrate on playing golf as well as he can," McCormack said. "It is very easy to get involved in a whole bunch of other things. Sports personalities often think if they are a champion in sport they can be a champion at everything else. They just think they can do everything, and they can't. Tiger knows that. There will be a time for all those things later on if he so chooses."[87]

Tiger and his parents agree. "We are not a greedy family," said his mother. "We're not the type of family to sell our son to get a lot of money." Tiger said, "The real issue is that if I'm spread too thin with a lot of endorsements, then my golf is going to suffer. That's what I don't want to happen."[88]

Tiger the CEO

Despite IMG's help, Tiger must still spend a great deal of time managing his affairs as chief executive officer (CEO) of ETW, Inc., the corporation formed to shield his assets. He moved to Florida because it has no state income tax and bought a private jet to make travel easier. Tiger and his father also created the Tiger Woods Foundation, which he started with a $500,000 contribution, to promote opportunities for minorities in golf.

Tiger began learning early how to manage his own affairs; by age sixteen he was making travel arrangements for tournaments, booking hotels, and setting up practice times on his own. And although Earl Woods said learning to run a large corporation has been a difficult educational experience for his son, something even his business courses at Stanford could not prepare him for, he loves the challenges of the business world.

"Being CEO has its advantages," he said in *Black Enterprise.* "I make the overall decisions, while people that I can absolutely trust, like my dad, go out and do the legwork. These are people who will not do anything contradictory to what I believe in. And everything is run through me before anything is finalized."[89]

Tiger's economic impact on golf has extended far beyond his own pocketbook. His attendance at a tournament after the Masters now brought in an additional $250,000 to $400,000 in ticket sales and sent television ratings soaring to new heights, a major factor in the lucrative new four-year contract the PGA signed in 1997 to televise its events on six different networks. The Western Open, for instance, had a television audience more than twice as large as the previous year.

A *Sports Illustrated* article in September 1997 claimed that in his first year as a pro, Tiger was responsible for a $150 million increase in course fees and sales of merchandise, a $60 million (100 percent) jump in Nike golf apparel and footwear sales, and a $343 million (100 percent) increase in television contracts. Calling him a "cash machine," the magazine said, "Tiger Woods has generated an estimated $653.4 million for the PGA Tour, golf industry and himself since turning pro."[90]

The December 1 issue of *Forbes* magazine listed the forty richest athletes in the world based on estimated income for 1997. Michael Jordan of the Chicago Bulls was first with $78.3 million and Tiger was sixth at $26.1 million. The magazine, however, said earnings for athletes it listed were very likely far higher because its figures did not include income from side businesses.

Father and son share a laugh at a May 1997 news conference where Tiger Woods announced he would be a spokesman for American Express credit cards.

New Lifestyle, New Friends

Demands on Tiger's time increased tremendously—golf outings to raise money for his foundation, business meetings, making commercials, dealing with the news media, and practicing and playing more golf than ever. He was so much in demand that he complained, "Why does everyone want a piece of me?"[91]

But Tiger also began to reap the benefits of his huge success. He bought a luxurious condo in Isleworth, the exclusive, gated community in Orlando, Florida that is also home to sports celebrities like golfers Mark O'Meara and Lee Janzen; Michael Jordan, the greatest player in the history of basketball; and Ken Griffey Jr. of the Seattle Mariners. Tiger had actually known O'Meara since December 1991 when they played golf together in a meeting arranged by IMG and O'Meara dazzled Tiger with his fine putting.

Despite his newfound wealth, Tiger still likes getting together with old friends like Jerry Chang, his Stanford teammate, and activities enjoyed by most young people—a fact that amazed writers at the Masters, one of whom wrote:

> Away from the golf course, Woods didn't look much like a god. He ate burgers and fries, played Ping-Pong and P-I-G with his buddies, screamed at video games and drove his parents to the far end of their rented house. Michael Jordan called and Nike czar Phil Knight came by, and the Fed Exes and telegrams from across the world piled up on the coffee table, but none of it seemed to matter. What did matter was the Mortal Kombat video game and the fact that he was Motaro and . . . Chang was Kintaro and he had just ripped Kintaro's mutant head off and now there was green slime spewing out and Tiger could roar in his best creature voice, "Mmmmmmwaaaannnnnnggh."[92]

Tiger freely admits he sometimes yearns for his simpler life as an amateur:

> I miss college. I miss hanging out with my friends, getting in a little trouble. I have to be so guarded now. I miss sitting around drinking beer and talking half the night. There's no one my own age to hang out with anymore because almost

everyone my age is in college. I'm a target for everybody now, and there's nothing I can do about it. My mother was right when she said that turning pro would take away my youth. But golfwise, there was nothing left for me in college.[93]

Because players on the tour are all older, Tiger often takes Chang and other friends to tournaments so he can relax with someone his own age. When Tiger went to the 1997 British Open, he and his friends went first to the Mediterranean for a few days of fun in the sun. His father calls them the Rat Pack, a name first given to the group of friends famed singer Frank Sinatra socialized with.

Many of Tiger's newer friends are celebrities to whom he has turned for advice on how to handle his overwhelming fame and fortune. One of his closest new pals is Michael Jordan, who he calls "M." "He's taken me under his wing and he's tried to help out because I think he's one of the few people in this world who can identify with what I'm going through," Tiger said. "He deals with it everywhere he goes. I foresee us being great friends for the rest of our lives."[94]

Mark O'Meara

Although a few golfers on tour were jealous of his success and fame, most welcomed Tiger because they realized he would elevate the visibility and status of professional golf. His closest friend in golf is Mark O'Meara, an Isleworth neighbor he practices and spends time with by going to the movies or bass fishing. They make a stark contrast—cool, hip Tiger and the slightly pudgy, balding, forty-one-year-old O'Meara.

"My best friend on Tour is nineteen years older than me. And that's kind of tough," Tiger says. "He's married and he likes to do some weird stuff, but he can't do all the stuff a 22-year-old likes to do."[95] The friendship is beneficial for both; O'Meara has helped Tiger adapt to the PGA tour while Tiger's youthful enthusiasm and competitive drive have rejuvenated the older golfer.

Despite his friend's success, O'Meara realizes Tiger has become a prisoner of his celebrity. "I wouldn't want to be Tiger Woods," he said. "I can still go to the Olive Garden and have dinner and nobody bothers me."[96]

The friendship did not stop them from battling down the stretch in February 1997 for the title in the Pebble Beach National Pro-Am. Tiger shot 63 and 64 in the final two rounds and birdied the last three holes to come within a stroke of catching O'Meara.

Tiger's heroic 267-yard three-wood second shot that made the green on the difficult par-5 eighteenth hole, which no golfer is supposed to be able to reach in two swings, set him up for his final birdie and produced an unbelievable, deafening roar from fans. But his new friend shrugged off the ear-splitting eruption of Tigermania.

"[It] just motivated me more," said O'Meara, who answered with birdies on the final two holes to win the tournament for the fifth time. "I was pretty jacked to beat him," admitted O'Meara. "Maybe I didn't knock the flags down like my little guy Tiger Woods did, but I stayed focused and held my composure." For Tiger it was a bittersweet loss. "I think it's great Mark won," Woods said. "I love him to death. But I'm disappointed [not to win]."[97]

Tiger's Racial Identity

Shortly after turning professional, Tiger helped start a new national debate about race in America. Three factors figured in the new awareness about race: his first Nike advertisement, an appearance on the *Oprah Winfrey* television show after the Masters, and racially insensitive comments by golfer Frank "Fuzzy" Zoeller.

The controversial Nike ad, which appeared within days after he turned professional, ended with Tiger saying: "There are still courses in the U.S. I am not allowed to play because of the color of my skin. Hello World. I've heard I'm not ready for you. Are you ready for me?"[98]

Some news commentators charged Nike was trying to benefit from the nation's racial divide, charging that the statement was ludicrous because any country club would be honored to have him as a guest. The fact remains, however, that Tiger felt he was denied playing privileges at navy courses as a youngster because of his race. In addition, many whites-only courses still bar other young black golfers from their courses.

In defending the ad Tiger said: "People have been so afraid to admit that golf has had a problem dealing with minorities and

One Golfer's "Fuzzy" Thinking

The "joke" that Fuzzy Zoeller told about Tiger Woods during the final round of the Masters highlighted the great racial divide that exists in America between the two races. In a *Time* magazine story about Tiger's racial makeup, Jack E. White writes that Zoeller, like many whites, was guilty of failing to understand the current racial climate.

> "His real crime was not, as he and his defenders seem to think, merely a distasteful breach of racial etiquette or an inept attempt at humor. The real crime was falling behind the times. The old black and white stereotypes are out of date, and Zoeller is just the latest casualty of America's failure to come to grips with the perplex and rapidly evolving significance of racial identity in what is fast becoming the most polyglot society in history."

White also claimed Zoeller had not seen Tiger as "the new king of golf, through whose veins runs the blood of four continents" but the black stereotype of a "fried-chicken-and-collard-greens-eating Sambo."

Although Zoeller apologized—"My comments were not intended to be racially derogatory, and I apologize for the fact that they were misconstrued in that fashion," he said—he paid a stiff price for his fuzzy thinking. K Mart quickly dropped him as spokesman for its golf equipment, he lost other lucrative endorsements, and he was attacked by the media for months.

The resulting debate, however, may have done some good by making whites consider the tastelessness of jokes they make about blacks.

Frank "Fuzzy" Zoeller adjusts his sunglasses during a round of golf. The furor over his remarks about Tiger Woods at the Masters also made Zoeller adjust his attitude about black golfers.

have always excluded them. Well, I'm sorry, but the mistake was to exclude them. What [the ad] did was make people talk about it. That's where change happens. You have to make people aware of the situation and they start talking about it. It shook the golf world a little bit but it shook it in the direction it needed to be shaken."[99]

The resulting furor led to a national dialogue about his race, including whether Tiger should be considered black or Asian. The news media had always referred to Tiger as black while mentioning, sometimes, that his mother was from Thailand. Tiger had always known that in America, a nation preoccupied and divided by race, anyone of black ancestry was always considered black. He had accepted that designation by the media when he was younger, but as Tiger grew older and more famous he wanted the world to know he also valued his mother's Asian heritage, including the fact that he had adopted her Buddhist religion. "I like Buddhism because it's a whole way of being and living," he says. "It's based on discipline and respect and personal responsibility. I like Asian culture better than [America's] because of that. It's how my mother raised me."[100]

In an appearance on *Oprah Winfrey*, Tiger heated up the controversy by admitting it bothered him to be referred to *only* as black. "It does. Growing up, I came up with this name; I'm Cablinasian."[101] The phrase reflected his true ethnic makeup: Caucasian, black, American Indian, Thai, and Chinese.

Zoeller, who has won both the Masters and the U.S. Open and is known for his easygoing nature and waggish sense of humor, always tries to leave his audience laughing. But a tasteless joke he made while Tiger was still putting the finishing touches on his record-setting Masters triumph had a mildly racist overtone. It touched off an incident when it was aired nationally a week later by the CNN television network.

In the transcript CNN released Zoeller, who had already completed his round, said, "That little boy [Woods] is driving well, and he's putting well. He's doing everything it takes to win. So, you know what you guys do when he gets in here? You pat him on the back and say congratulations and enjoy it and tell him not to serve fried chicken next year. Got it?" On the videotape Zoeller

A dapper Tiger Woods appears with Oprah Winfrey on her show in April 1997. His remarks during the show contributed to the debate about race that swirled around him for much of that year.

then snapped his fingers, turned to walk away, and added, "Or collard greens or whatever the hell they serve." [102]

Zoeller was trying to joke about what Tiger would order for next year's traditional Masters banquet for past champions. But many people felt the phrases "boy" and "they" and the references to foods associated with black culture were, if not racist, at the very least paternalistic and degrading to blacks.

The comments created a firestorm even though Zoeller quickly apologized and was defended by many of his fellow golfers, who said he was not a racist and was simply being Fuzzy by making a joke, even if it was tasteless.

Is Tiger Black?

Because Tiger has become a powerful symbol of minority success, some blacks worry he is turning his back on them by demanding that other parts of his racial heritage be honored as well.

In *Christianity Today,* Chris Rice writes that in Tiger blacks see "a man proud of his multiethnic heritage who . . . speaks candidly about racial discrimination" and is as big a hero to the black community as heavyweight champion Joe Louis decades earlier:

> For them, each thunderous punch against the Brown Bomber's German opponent was a declaration of war, just as each Woods birdie was an "I told you so" to a system that had attempted to lock him out, and each 300-yard drive an arrow to the soul of America, proving a point . . . [and crowning] Tiger Woods not as a symbol of America's inherent racial goodness, but the inherent evil that blacks must overcome to achieve."[103]

In *Essence*, Isabel Wilkerson says blacks "pretended not to notice that he had a Thai mother and disregarded the Native American and Caucasian he said was in him."[104] She also notes that the connotation "black" has little to do with skin color or genetics and everything to do with making "a political statement, a cultural declaration."[105]

In *Ebony* magazine, Hugh B. Price, president of the National Urban League, counters that "the critical thing is he not be in denial about any particular aspect of his heritage. He doesn't deny his Black roots. Nor does he—or should he—deny the heritage of his mother, who is Thai, or whatever ethnic roots may be in his background."[106]

For Tiger, any argument about his race is academic: "I'm just who I am, whoever you see in front of you."[107]

Chapter 6

Tiger Woods: Greatest Golfer Ever?

Wᴴᴇɴ Cᴜʀᴛɪs Sᴛʀᴀɴɢᴇ interviewed Tiger Woods during the telecast of the Greater Milwaukee Open, Tiger surprised the two-time U.S. Open champion by saying he expected to win every time he played. "If you're not going to a tournament to win," Tiger said, "there's really no point. That's the attitude I've had all my life, that's the attitude I will always have." Strange then told him that many golfers are happy to finish second or third because it means a good pay day. "That's not too bad," Tiger admitted, "but I want to win. That's just my nature." With a sly little grin, Strange told him, "You'll learn." [108]

Tiger astonished the golf world by winning three of his first nine tournaments, capturing his first major at the Masters, and setting a tour record for earnings in 1997 with slightly over $2 million. That same year he also became the number-one-ranked golfer in the world, won PGA Player of the Year honors, and was the first golfer since Lee Trevino in 1971 named Associated Press Male Athlete of the Year.

But Tiger eventually learned Strange had been right.

Tiger failed to win again in 1997 after his victory in the Western Open in July. Worse, after all the talk following the Masters about his chances of becoming the first golfer to sweep the four majors in a single year for a grand slam, Tiger finished in ties for nineteenth in the U.S. Open, twenty-fourth in the British Open, and twenty-ninth in the PGA Championship. In December, Tiger also stumbled in his first Ryder Cup competition at Valderrama, Spain, posting a disappointing 1-3-1 match play record as the

Europeans beat the Americans by a single point in the biennial competition.

"Golf humbles you every day, every shot, really," Tiger could now admit. "I know how hard the game is." [109]

News Media—Friend and Foe

From the time Tiger captured the attention of the news media while belting drives as a toddler in diapers, he received positive, almost worshipful coverage. Reporters delighted in telling the world about the young golfer's amazing accomplishments, the story behind his nickname, and how a young black man was becoming king in a sport with roots in whites-only country clubs. The media spread the legend of Tiger Woods throughout the world, making him famous and enabling him to sign endorsement contracts worth millions of dollars.

But the news media have always taken a paradoxical approach to the celebrities they create. Once they have made stars out of previously unknown athletes, actors, or singers, reporters start looking for flaws in the golden public images they themselves have helped manufacture and polish.

Tiger Woods eyes a putt during the 1996 Ryder Cup in Valderrama, Spain. Although touted as the star of the U.S. team, his mediocre play contributed to an American loss in the match against European golfers.

Tiger and the Media

Tiger Woods says "blowing my nose is not exactly an event." The problem is that many reporters will write about the most insignificant things that happen to someone as famous as he is.

In their zeal to find out something new about Tiger, reporters sometimes ask questions that sound silly, like the query from the reporter at the 1998 British Open who piped up with, "Did you ever play soccer as a boy?" "I wish I could figure out what that has to do with golf," said a quizzical Tiger. "It interests me," said the questioner. Whether the question was stupid or not, Tiger admitted he played soccer when he was young.

The question seemed reasonable to a reporter from a country in which soccer is the top sport, but to Tiger it seemed a waste of time. And when it comes to Tiger's time, the media has an insatiable appetite. He is besieged daily with requests for interviews and during 1998 was forced to hold full-scale interviews before every tournament to satisfy that hunger. But at the World Series of Golf in Akron, Ohio, in late August, Tiger said the weekly sessions would end. "It really makes no sense to do it every single week. It's almost become an obligation," he complained. "You've seen it," Tiger told one reporter, "you've been out here, for what, the last three or four weeks now? It's the same ones, same questions [over and over]."

In that same interview Tiger said he did not think "blowing my nose" was news. The problem is that to reporters anything *new* about Tiger automatically becomes hot copy because he has so many fans who want to know *everything* about him.

Tiger also resents it when reporters use news conferences about golf tournaments to pry into his personal life. He usually ignores such questions but did offer an answer at the World Series of Golf when a reporter said, "Tiger, this is for the ladies. If you're dating, how has that affected your life?"

"I am dating and it's—it's been very nice and very difficult, too, at times because I haven't had the time to devote as much time as I'd like to in relationships because I'm traveling so much," Tiger said. "It's very difficult to get know somebody. But I'm very pleased with some of the friendships I've made and the people I've gotten to know and that's only to continue as I get used my to life out here. And maybe I can find someone that can fit into this life."

The question had no more to do with golf than the query about soccer. Dealing with the media is just part of the price of fame Tiger pays every day of his life.

"Life in the media spotlight can be both exhilarating and exasperating—a blessing and curse," says Earl Woods. "Just ask so many of our world's celebrities who have been scorched by probing eyes intent on denigrating reputations and exposing private lives."[110] Woods himself has had problems dealing with the media: He has been criticized for forcing his son to play golf from the time he was an infant, ridiculed for outrageous statements about how Tiger will change the world, and questioned about why he and Kultida, although still married, began living in separate homes after their son turned professional.

Tiger began to experience this second, darker side of fame while still an amateur. After a Monday practice round in his first Masters, Tiger turned down requests for interviews because he had already scheduled a news conference for the next day. He wanted to limit distractions so he could concentrate on golf but some reporters, hungry for any news about the teen sensation, accused him of being arrogant for refusing to talk to them.

Members of the media also cynically questioned his thank-you note to Masters officials, which they claimed was written to polish his image. Scott Ostler of the *San Francisco Chronicle* voiced a minority opinion when he wrote that the letter and free clinic the Woodses conducted at a local golf course where blacks played "smack ominously of a father instilling values in his son." [111]

In the summer of 1996 the media had a field day speculating about when Tiger would turn professional and how much he would collect in endorsements. It bothered Tiger that ABC golf commentator Brent Musburger reported he was turning pro without having interviewed him. "He knows more about my life than I do," complained Tiger. "He's never asked me anything." [112] The fact that Musburger was right was irrelevant; Tiger resented the intrusion into his life.

"A Packaged Product"

Reporters thought it was cute when Tiger chirped "hello, world" to open his news conference at the Greater Milwaukee Open and most used the quote in their stories. But when Nike ads based on that theme soon appeared, they angrily claimed Tiger had used them to jump-start Nike's campaign.

Tiger, wrote Tim Rosaforte, "was no longer the amateur golfer who hit scruffy two-piece balls out of plastic milk crates at Stanford . . . [but] a packaged product, a corporation, and an icon" and declared "the age of Tiger Woods' innocence had ended." [113] Reporters at the news conference also noted in their stories how many Nike "swoosh" designs, the firm's corporate logo, adorned his clothing as well as that of his father and mother.

The millions of dollars Tiger made simply by signing a few contracts ignited a flood of negative stories that said no one was worth such huge sums and questioned his long relationship with International Management Group, the company that now managed his career. IMG had courted him for several years, arranging meetings for Tiger with other clients like Arnold Palmer and Greg Norman, and even putting his father on its payroll as a "scout" to assess junior golfers.

Tiger began to learn how fickle the media's affection could be when the criticism quickly turned to gushing praise when he began to dominate the PGA tour as no rookie ever had. But coverage turned nasty again in late September when Tiger, pleading exhaustion after winning his third U.S. Amateur and playing four straight tour events, withdrew from the Buick Challenge in Pine Mountain, Georgia.

The media attacked him as never before because he also skipped a dinner in his honor during the Buick Open to give

The huge sums Tiger Woods makes from endorsement deals have changed the way the news media treats him. Once considered a heroic young amateur, many reporters began to view him as an arrogant millionaire.

Tiger and his Dad

From the time Tiger Woods was two months old and his father would hold him high in the palm of his hand in an attempt to make him work on improving his balance, balance being essential to a good golf swing. Tiger had always been considered a creation of his father. But their relationship has always been close and loving, more like good friends than father and son.

In *A Biography of Tiger Woods,* author John Strege writes that when Tiger was fourteen he said his dad was "the coolest guy I know." They rarely had problems and when Tiger needed to talk, his father always made time to listen. "Tiger's relationship with his father had always been void of the Richter Scale activity that most sons and fathers encounter during the teen years," writes Strege. "The first time he overindulged at a fraternity party, Tiger got sick and humbly told the story to his father. Rather than getting angry, Earl told him he could maintain control by drinking spacers of water or soda between beers. This was the kind of interaction the two shared, and it explains Tiger's respectful, mature behavior even as a kid."

But after Tiger became a professional, that relationship changed. Tiger began living his own life and making his own decisions; it was simply the coming-of-age process everyone goes through as they get older. In an interview in early 1998 Tiger said he is now on his own: "I am a visitor in my parents' house. It's been that way since I left Stanford."

him the Fred Haskins Award. Realizing he had made a mistake, Tiger rescheduled the dinner for November and made a heartfelt apology. "I should've attended the dinner," he said when he finally received the award. "I admit I was wrong, and I'm sorry for any inconvenience I may have caused. But I have learned from that, and will never make that mistake again."[114] But the media damage had already been done: Some people now viewed Tiger as an arrogant, spoiled young millionaire.

Even the euphoria over his historic Masters victory was diluted when he turned down President Bill Clinton's request to attend a celebration two days later in New York to honor the fiftieth anniversary of Jackie Robinson's debut with the Brooklyn Dodgers. John Feinstein, whose *The First Coming: Tiger Woods: Master or Martyr?* catalogues every miscue he believes Earl or Tiger Woods ever made, wrote that "forty-eight hours after handling himself so magnificently at Augusta . . . Tiger had blown off the memory of the man who had blazed more trails than anyone [for black athletes]."[115]

When Tiger lost his invincibility on the golf course in the second half of 1997, writers questioned whether his ability had been overhyped. But he was still besieged with requests for interviews and his every move on or off the golf course was microscopically examined. Tiger was usually restrained and guarded in interviews and the one time he let down his guard, it was a complete disaster.

A story by Charles P. Pierce in the April 1997 edition of *Gentleman's Quarterly* created a sensation by reporting that Tiger laced his language in private with profanity and liked telling off-color jokes, behavior that contrasted starkly with his choirboy image. Actually, it was not much of a revelation that a twenty-one-year-old would swear or laugh at such humor. Tiger was angry that the article focused almost exclusively on those two topics and believed he had been ambushed by the reporter.

"Look," said Mark McCormack, founder of IMG. "Tiger was twenty-one-years old. The crew at the GQ photo shoot started telling jokes and Tiger joined in. Tiger believed that he was speaking off the record. He will learn. We all learn." [116]

The lesson Tiger learned was to keep his mouth shut. After that article Tiger restricted his one-on-one interviews and became more wary than ever about answering questions.

A Not So Spectacular 1998

Tiger began 1998 in spectacular fashion with a victory in the Johnnie Walker Classic, a PGA European Tour event in Thailand. Although he trailed South African Ernie Els by eleven strokes after the first two rounds, he rallied to tie the two-time U.S. Open champion with a final round 65. When Tiger beat Els on the second playoff hole, it looked like he was ready to resume his domination of the PGA tour. He then finished tied for second in the Mercedes Championship in January, the first tournament of the year, and second in the Nissan Open in March when he lost a playoff to Billy Mayfair.

In April the media was predicting another Masters victory, but Tiger finished eighth, six strokes behind Mark O'Meara. Instead of donning the green jacket for the second straight year, he helped his best friend on tour slip into the winner's coat. "I'm forty-one-years-old, I can't get my arm way up there,"[117] O'Meara joked while struggling into the coveted winner's blazer.

Ironically Woods, whose reputation had always been based on being the youngest golfer to take center stage at tournaments, was paired the first round with nineteen-year-old Matt Kuchar, the Georgia Tech sophomore who had succeeded him as U.S. Amateur champion. Kuchar shot even par for four rounds and won the hearts of millions with his brilliant smile and open joy at playing in the Masters. At age twenty-two, Tiger was no longer a child prodigy but a star being challenged by younger golfers.

Tiger won the BellSouth Classic in his next start, but it was his only tour victory of the season. When he could manage only a tie for eighteenth in the U.S. Open in June, he was winless in the last five majors and reporters suggested that Tiger had lost his roar. Associated Press sportswriter Doug Ferguson wrote:

So much for all that talk about a Grand Slam. These days, Tiger Woods would be happy just to get into contention at a major championship. Once again, he found little reason to smile Sunday [June 16] at the U.S. Open. "I'm disappointed," Woods said after taking three straight bogeys early on, then three-putting the 18th

With an adoring crowd looking on, Tiger Woods hits a shot at the 1997 Masters en route to his first major title.

from about 8 feet for a 73 that left him at 10-over 290 for the tournament. "I came here to win, and I just didn't do it." Lately, Woods hasn't even come close, a far cry from the expectations of a year ago. [118]

However, Tiger came out snarling at the British Open in July, shooting a 5-under-par 65 at Royal Birkdale Golf Club in Southport, England, for a share of the first round lead. Although he cooled off with rounds of 73 and 77, Tiger shot 66 on the final day to thrill the crowd, finishing with a spectacular thirty-foot chip-in from just off the seventeenth green and a thirty-foot putt at the eighteenth for a 281. It looked as though another of Tiger's patented charges might be enough for victory but he finished third, a stroke back of O'Meara and little-known Brian Watts to just miss joining them in a three-hole playoff for the title. O'Meara beat Watts for his second major of the season.

A More Mature Golfer

Though Tiger finished third at the British Open, he finally seemed to have regained his magic touch. Gary Van Sickle wrote in Sports Illustrated that "Tiger Woods took a giant step in his evolution as a golfer." He praised Woods for being more patient, having a more controlled swing, and being more mature in his judgment. Tiger agreed. "It's an evolution every player goes through. It's learning how to play golf," [119] he said.

Tiger was upstaged again by another teen sensation at the British Open when seventeen-year-old Justin Rose of England shot a second round 66 and finished tied for fourth, one shot behind Tiger. After Rose's 66 an English newspaper headline read: "British lion, 17, mauls Tiger"—a reference to the fact that Rose's score was 66, seven shots better than Tiger's 73. Rose also tied Tiger for the low round by an amateur in a British Open but because it came under much more difficult weather conditions, rain and fierce winds, Tiger graciously commented, "My 66 was nowhere near as good because mine was in calm weather." [120]

In the last major tournament of the year, the PGA Championship in August at Sahalee Country Club in Redmond, Washington, Tiger came out smoking again with a 66. But he faded with three rounds in the 70s and finished tied for tenth in a tournament won by Vijay Singh of Fiji. After his brilliant first round, Tiger was asked if he was satisfied with his season.

"Well, overall, I've played really well this entire year. People ask me why am I in a slump. I'm really not in a slump," he argued.

I've been playing well. I've been right there in majors. I had a chance at the Masters going into Sunday. Didn't quite fire a low enough round. Had a really good shot at the British Open. Came up one shot short of a play-off. So I've been close to putting it all together and being in the hunt where I could legitimately win. It's about getting the right breaks at the right time. So overall I'm very pleased the way I've played this year in the majors, even though I haven't won. I've given it everything I've got. I just came up short.[121]

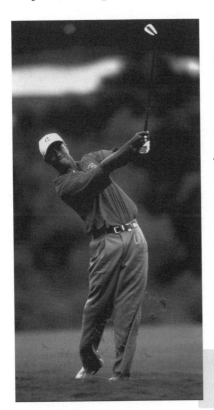

Tiger also displayed his tantalizing yet infuriating (to his fans) habit in 1998 of playing well but failing to win in two important tournaments in Great Britain in October. First he teamed with O'Meara and John Daly as the U.S. entry in the Dunhill Cup, a series of matches between teams from sixteen different countries. The American threesome breezed through the opening rounds at St. Andrews in Scotland only to lose a semifinal match to Spain. Woods, undefeated until then,

Tiger Woods hits a shot as a member of the U.S. team at the 1997 Ryder Cup in Spain.

lost his match by a stroke to Santiago Luna when Tiger missed a four-foot putt on the final hole. Daly won but O'Meara also lost and the U.S. team was eliminated.

Looking dominant again the next week in the World Match Play Championship in Virginia Water, England, Tiger easily advanced to the final match October 18, where, ironically, he met O'Meara, his friend and mentor. O'Meara rallied from four holes back in the 36-hole finale to beat Tiger 1-up, making a fifteen-foot birdie putt on the final hole to clinch the title. Tiger, waiting to try a birdie putt of his own, a putt that was now no longer relevant to the outcome, rushed over and embraced O'Meara.

"I'm very happy for Mark," said Tiger. "He's still my friend no matter what. But we're playing competitors and I wanted to win the tournament as much as he did. I know that, he knows that." Another bad day with the putter had sealed his fate once again. Tiger three-putted on the thirty-fourth hole for bogey to give O'Meara a one-hole lead he never relinquished. "I hit a bad putt, I pushed it, and I pushed the second one coming back,"[122] Tiger said.

Even after his loss to O'Meara, Tiger found it hard to understand why he was not winning more tournaments because he believes he is playing better. "I can't even describe how much better of a player I am physically and mentally," he said. "The shots I can hit now, there's no way I could have played last year."[123]

Tiger won $1.8 million on the PGA tour in 1998 to finish fourth on the money list, had thirteen top ten finishes, the best of any golfer on tour, and was second in both average driving distance (296.3 yards) and scoring average (69.21). Putting was Tiger's downfall throughout 1998, a fact borne out by his 147th ranking in putting. A year earlier he had been 60th in putting and the extra strokes proved costly.

Woods lost the battle for the Vardon Trophy for the scoring average title to David Duval in the Tour Championship, the final PGA event of 1998. Woods shot 289 for four rounds from October 29 to November 1 but Duval was seven strokes better to lower his scoring average for the season to 69.13. Duval also broke the record for tour earnings that Woods set in 1997 by collecting nearly $2.6 million.

In November 1998 Tiger got a free pass into the PGA Grand Slam of Golf, a match play event for winners of the four Grand Slam events. The tournament needed a fourth player because O'Meara had won two of the Grand Slams. Tiger made the most of the opportunity by beating PGA Champion Vijay Singh 2-up in the title match to win $400,000 and get a bit of consolation for not having won any of the four majors.

Playing in a howling wind and rain squalls at Poipu Bay Resort on the Hawaiian island of Kauai, Tiger took the lead for the first time on the 15th hole and clinched the tournament on the 17th with a 12-foot birdie putt. "It was a rough day," Woods admitted. "Conditions were awfully hard, very difficult, very demanding. You had to be very patient, execute the shots you had to execute and keep your patience. Today was one of those days if you lose your patience, you loose the match very quickly."[124]

The Greatest Golfer Ever?

Golf writers in 1998 spoke of Tiger's "slump" even though he was having a season that, by anyone else's standards, would have been considered terrific. The reason was that expectations have always been much higher for Tiger than for other golfers. And Tiger, because he expects so much of himself, has been as guilty of creating those inflated expectations as the news media or other golfers.

Tiger did it to himself by saying, over and over again, "I don't want to be the best black golfer, I want to be the best golfer ever."[125] Jack Nicklaus, who holds the unofficial title Tiger seeks, contributed to the problem at the 1996 Masters when he said: "Both Arnold [Palmer] and I agree that you could take my Masters [six] and his Masters [four] and add them together, and this kid should win more than that. He will be your favorite [in the Masters] for the next twenty years. If he isn't, there's something wrong."[126]

At the time some writers speculated Nicklaus's comments might create expectations Tiger could never hope to meet. But most reporters uncritically used them in their stories—they did, after all, make good copy—only to look silly when Tiger struggled and failed to make the cut.

Tiger Woods enjoys a round of golf at the 1996 Masters with two of the greatest players in the game's history, Arnold Palmer (left) and Jack Nicklaus (center).

However, members of the media are beginning to realize the excessive burden they have placed on Tiger's shoulders. In commenting on Tiger's new, more mature playing style at the PGA Championship, Associated Press sports columnist Jim Litke wrote, "If the rest of us [reporters] are going to continue to hold [Tiger] to a higher standard, we're also going to have to be patient enough to give him time to learn to play this game more like everybody else does." [127]

And Tiger believes he improved in his second full season on tour. "This is a—well, I have to say just—It's a more mature Tiger than you saw last year at this time," he said at the PGA Championship. "I've got more shots. I understand my game. It's just one of those things where over time, you just mature and you learn how to play golf." [128]

Tiger also admitted he became fatigued in the second half of his first season on tour in 1997 because he had never had to play so many tournaments or deal with so many requests for his time from the media and others. He said by managing his schedule more wisely, he will be able to play more consistently and at a higher level. "I was pretty tired because I wasn't used to playing that much golf," Tiger said at the World Series of Golf. "And this year, I feel very fresh [late in the season] because I've mixed up my schedule, had more breaks. Took some advice from other tour players and just kind of created a schedule in which I would be able to last the entire year." [129]

What Other Golfers Say About Tiger

The ultimate judges of Tiger Woods are his peers, the golfers he competes against in tournaments around the world. Here is a sampling of what they have said about him.

Jim Thorpe, winner of three PGA tour events and the only other black golfer on tour besides Tiger in the '90s, 1989 British Open champion Mark Calcavecchia, and 1988 PGA champion Jeff Sluman talked about Woods with the author at the 1998 Greater Milwaukee Open, which Sluman won.

Thorpe: "When Tiger came along, the stage had been set. Guys who went before him didn't get the recognition they deserved. Tiger is the fruit from the seed that was planted years ago by other golfers. I'm very happy for him."

Calcavecchia: "[Tiger's popularity] is good for everyone. I saw his picture in the mall the other day, on a big stand about ten feet high. I was thinking, 'Man, this guy is all over the place.' In fact, he probably doesn't even know how big he is in the world of professional sports. The interest level [in golf] has gone up, there's more fans than ever before, and the prize money is going up. Everything is going in the right direction and I know a lot has to be attributed to him."

Sluman: "He's meant a lot to golf. We always need great players and he certainly is one. He has the potential to be one of the best of all time. We're fortunate to have him."

Paul Azinger, 1993 PGA champion, said in a story in *Sports Illustrated for Kids*: "He's Michael Jordan in long pants."

Tom Lehman, 1996 British Open champion, commenting in *Sports Illustrated* magazine on Tiger's Masters victory: "He was phenomenal. He threw down the gauntlet and said, 'This is golf in the twenty-first century.'"

Jack Nicklaus told *Fortune* magazine: "If he continues to win—and win majors, which is what he has to do—his impact on the game can be much greater than mine. When you combine that with today's intense media coverage and his ethnicity, it means he has the opportunity to attract new people to the game, and it's all good, all good."

Johnny Miller, NBC analyst and winner of the U.S. Open and British Open, said in *Sports Illustrated*, "It wouldn't surprise me if he wins fifty tournaments and twelve majors. Tiger said we haven't seen the best of him yet, and he's right. I think he's got a big agenda."

It is performing at a high level for an entire career that Tiger has to worry about, not just an "entire year." Nicklaus won two amateur majors, eighteen professional majors, and a hundred tournaments overall in a career that spanned five decades and was still going strong in 1998. By age twenty-two Nicklaus had three majors (two U.S. Amateurs and a U.S. Open) to four for Tiger (three U.S. Amateurs and a Masters) but from age twenty-three to twenty-seven he won six more—three Masters, a second U.S. Open, a British Open, and a PGA Championship.

Tiger has his work cut out for him, but he has, after all, only just begun his career, and challenges and high expectations are something he has never feared. "So far I've been able to perform when it counts," Tiger has said. "I'm like my dad in that we both get icy under pressure. I don't want to sound cocky, but that's what I love the most—doing it when it counts the most. That's what I play for, not the money." [130]

Hale Irwin, the three-time U.S. Open champion who won twenty PGA tour events and went on to be a big winner as well on the Senior PGA tour, says it will take years to put Tiger's career into proper perspective. "He's still a young man," says Irwin. "Let's let him grow, naturally develop, before we pass judgment on him, saying that he's the best who ever played. Let's give the young man a chance to establish his own identity and establish his own success. And let's go along for the ride and enjoy it with him." [131]

Another Kind of Greatness?

Although his impact on golf has already been immense, the question of how great his impact will be outside the sport remains. It is doubtful Tiger will ever live up to the claims of his father that he will be some sort of savior of mankind, but as a person of color and a role model for the young, Tiger can have a huge impact on American culture for decades to come.

America is a nation that reveres its sports stars but all too often becomes disillusioned when they use drugs, beat their spouses, or get into other kinds of trouble. Tiger Woods considers himself a role model for many young people, a job he takes very seriously.

"I grew up in the media's eye but I was taught never to lose sight of where I came from," he has said. "Athletes aren't as gentlemanly as they used to be. I don't like that change. I like the idea of being a role model. It's an honor. People took time to help me as a kid and they impacted my life. I want to do the same for kids."[132] He already works with kids through his Tiger Woods Foundation and reaches others through free golf clinics. In the future, he will doubtless have many other opportunities to help young people.

At a golf clinic in Dallas, Tiger Woods teaches a youngster to swing a golf club.

Some observers also believe his easy acceptance of his racial identity can be a healing factor on the divisive issue of race, which has bedeviled America for its entire history. In an article in *Time* magazine in 1997 on Tiger's racial makeup, American University sociologist Amitai Etzioni says allowing people to glory in their ethnic diversity "has the potential to soften the racial lines that now divide America by rendering them more like economic differences and less like harsh, almost immutable cast lines." Conservative analyst Douglas Besharov of the American Enterprise Institute agrees, saying a more ambiguous identity for mixed-race children might be "the best hope for the future of American (race) relations."[133]

For Tiger Woods, the future may hold as many victories in these areas as he scores on a golf course. But as with his greatness on the golf course, only time will tell.

Notes

Introduction: From Child Prodigy to Superstar

1. Quoted in Gary Smith, "The Chosen One," *Sports Illustrated*, December 23, 1996, p. 31.
2. Quoted in Roy S. Johnson, "Tiger! The Sky's the Limit for Golf—the Game and the Business," *Fortune*, May 12, 1997, p. 74.

Chapter 1: A Champion Made, Not Born

3. Earl Woods with Pete McDaniel, *Training a Tiger: A Father's Guide to Raising a Winner in Both Golf and Life*. New York: HarperCollins, 1997, p. 23.
4. Quoted in John Strege, *Tiger: A Biography of Tiger Woods*. New York: Broadway Books, 1997, p. 26.
5. Quoted in Earl Woods with Fred Mitchell, *Playing Through: Straight Talk on Hard Work, Big Dreams, and Adventures with Tiger*. New York: HarperCollins, 1998, p. xi.
6. Woods with Mitchell, *Playing Through*, p. 6.
7. Woods with Mitchell, *Playing Through*, p. 14.
8. Quoted in Tim Rosaforte, *Tiger Woods: The Makings of a Champion*. New York: St. Martin's Press, 1997, p. 12.
9. Quoted in Strege, *Tiger*, p. 9.
10. Woods with Mitchell, *Playing Through*, p. 57.
11. Woods with Mitchell, *Playing Through*, p. 51.
12. Woods with McDaniel, *Training a Tiger*, p. xvii.
13. Quoted in Strege, *Tiger*, p. 11.

Chapter 2: Early Success and Fame

14. Quoted in Rosaforte, *Tiger Woods*, p. 15.
15. Quoted in Rick Reilly, "Goodness Gracious, He's a Great

Ball of Fire," *Sports Illustrated*, March 27, 1995, p. 66.

16. Quoted in Rosaforte, *Tiger Woods*, p. 17.

17. Quoted in Woods with Mitchell, *Playing Through*, p. 74.

18. *Tiger Woods: Son, Hero, and Champion*, Trans World International, CBS Video, 1997.

19. Quoted in Jeff Savage, *Tiger Woods: King of the Course*. Minneapolis: Lerner, 1998, p. 20.

20. *Tiger Woods: Son, Hero, and Champion*.

21. Quoted in John Strege, "Tiger Woods Has Everyone's Attention. He's Talented, He's Exciting, He's Grrreat!" *Sports Illustrated for Kids*, August 1997, p. 38.

22. Quoted in Woods with Mitchell, *Playing Through*, p. 83.

23. *Tiger Woods: Son, Hero, and Champion*.

24. Quoted in Strege, *Tiger*, p. 21.

25. Quoted in William Durbin, *Tiger Woods*. Philadelphia: Chelsea House, 1998, p. 23.

26. Quoted in Durbin, *Tiger Woods*, p. 23.

27. Woods with McDaniel, *Training a Tiger*, p. 149.

28. *Tiger Woods: Son, Hero, and Champion*.

29. Woods with McDaniel, *Training a Tiger*, p. 158.

30. Quoted in Rosaforte, *Tiger Woods*, p. 24.

31. Strege, *Tiger*, p. 10.

32. Quoted in Rosaforte, *Tiger Woods*, p. 22.

33. Quoted in Savage, *Tiger Woods*, p. 33.

Chapter 3: The Greatest Amateur Golfer Ever

34. Quoted in Rosaforte, *Tiger Woods*, p. 22.

35. Woods with Mitchell, *Playing Through*, p. 99.

36. Woods with Mitchell, *Playing Through*, p. 100.

37. Quoted in Rosaforte, *Tiger Woods*, p. 19.

38. Woods with Mitchell, *Playing Through*, p. 91.

39. Quoted in Curry Kirkpatrick, "A Tiger in the Grass," *Newsweek*, April 10, 1995, p. 72.

40. Woods with Mitchell, *Playing Through*, p. 90.

41. Quoted in John Garrity, *Tiger Woods: The Making of a Champion*. New York: Simon & Schuster, 1997, p. 6.

42. Quoted in Strege, *Tiger*, p. 35.

43. Quoted in Rosaforte, *Tiger Woods*, p. 27.

44. Quoted in Durbin, *Tiger Woods*, p. 10.

45. *Tiger Woods: Son, Hero, and Champion.*

46. Quoted in Strege, *Tiger*, p. 40.

47. Quoted in Garrity, *Tiger Woods*, p. 18.

48. Quoted in Rosaforte, *Tiger Woods*, p. 69.

49. Quoted in Strege, *Tiger*, p. 81.

50. Quoted in Rosaforte, *Tiger Woods*, p. 95.

51. Quoted in Tim Rosaforte, "The Comeback Kid," *Sports Illustrated*, September 5, 1994, p. 16.

52. Quoted in Garrity, *Tiger Woods*, p. 25.

Chapter 4: The Greatest Amateur Ever Turns Pro

53. Quoted in Curry Kirkpatrick, "Great Names, Great Games," *Newsweek*, December 26, 1994–January 2, 1995, p. 115.

54. Quoted in Kirkpatrick, "Great Names, Great Games," p. 115.

55. Quoted in Rick Reilly, "Strokes of Genius," *Sports Illustrated*, April 21, 1997, p. 35.

56. Quoted in Kirkpatrick, "A Tiger in the Grass," p. 70.

57. Quoted in Rosaforte, *Tiger Woods*, p. 121.

58. Quoted in Rick Reilly, "For You Harvey," *Sports Illustrated*, April 17, 1995, p. 20.

59. Quoted in Durbin, *Tiger Woods*, p. 42.

60. Quoted in Garrity, *Tiger Woods*, p. 44.

61. Quoted in Strege, *Tiger*, p. 109.

62. Quoted in Strege, *Tiger*, p. 71.

63. Woods with Mitchell, *Playing Through*, p. 155.

64. Quoted in Strege, *Tiger*, p. 101.

65. Quoted in Rosaforte, *Tiger Woods*, p. 125.

66. Woods with Mitchell, *Playing Through*, p. 192.

67. Quoted in Rosaforte, *Tiger Woods*, p. 104.

68. Quoted in Rosaforte, *Tiger Woods*, p. 141.

69. Quoted in Garrity, *Tiger Woods*, p. 72.

70. Quoted in Tom Callahan, "Is This Kid Superman?" *Golf Digest*, November 1996, p. 60.

71. Quoted in Rosaforte, *Tiger Woods*, p. 173.

72. Quoted in Gary D'Amato, "It's Official: Woods Era Dawns," *Milwaukee Journal-Sentinel*, August 29, 1996, p. C1.

73. Quoted in D'Amato, "It's Official," p. C3.

74. Quoted in Garrity, *Tiger Woods,* p. 74.

75. Quoted in D'Amato, "It's Official," p. C3.

76. Quoted in Gary D'Amato and Dan Manoyan, "Woods Says His Pro Golf Debut Was Successful," *Milwaukee Journal-Sentinel,* September 3, 1996, p. C13.

77. Quoted in Savage, *Tiger Woods,* p. 56.

78. Quoted in D'Amato, "It's Official," p. C3.

Chapter 5: A True Master of Golf

79. Quoted in Smith, "The Chosen One," p. 36.

80. Quoted in Rick Reilly, "Top Cat," *Sports Illustrated,* October 28, 1996, p. 48.

81. Reilly, "Top Cat," p. 48.

82. *Tiger Woods: Son, Hero, and Champion.*

83. Quoted in Woods with Mitchell, *Playing Through,* p. 165.

84. Quoted in Reilly, "Strokes of Genius," p. 49.

85. Quoted in Woods with Mitchell, *Playing Through,* p. 195.

86. Quoted in Ron Stodghill II et al., "Tiger, Inc.," *Business Week,* April 28, 1997, p. 32.

87. Quoted in John Barton, "Mark McCormack," *Golf Digest,* June 1998, p. 206.

88. Quoted in Stodghill et al., "Tiger, Inc.," p. 34.

89. Quoted in Eric L. Smith, "Eye of the Tiger," *Black Enterprise,* September 1997, p. 90.

90. Quoted in "Scorecard," *Sports Illustrated,* September 8, 1997, p. 21.

91. Quoted in Smith, "The Chosen One," p. 28.

92. Reilly, "Strokes of Genius," p. 39.

93. Quoted in Smith, "The Chosen One," p. 38.

94. Quoted in Tim Rosaforte, "Follow the Leader," *Golf World,* July 11, 1997, p. 22.

95. Quoted in Jonathan Abrahams, "Golden Child or Spoiled Brat?" *Golf Magazine,* April 1998, p. 60.

96. Quoted in Rosaforte, "Follow the Leader," p. 22.

97. Quoted in Jeff Rude, "Prince of Pebble, O'Meara Wins Despite Tiger on His Tail," *Golfweek,* February 8, 1997, p. 29.

98. Quoted in Rosaforte, *Tiger Woods,* p. 180.

99. *Tiger Woods: Son, Hero, and Champion.*

100. Quoted in Smith, "The Chosen One," p. 49.
101. Quoted in Jack E. White, "I'm Just Who I Am," *Time*, May 5, 1997, p. 34.
102. Quoted in White, "I'm Just Who I Am," p. 33.
103. Chris Rice, "Why Tiger Makes Us Feel Good: Is the Best Remedy for Racism Visible Black Achievement?" *Christianity Today*, July 14, 1997, p. 13.
104. Isabel Wilkerson, "The All American," *Essence*, November 1997, p. 99.
105. Wilkerson, "The All American," p. 102.
106. Quoted in Hugh B. Price et al., "Black America and Tiger's Dilemma," *Ebony*, July 1997, p. 32.
107. Quoted in White, "I'm Just Who I Am," p. 34.

Chapter 6: Tiger Woods: Greatest Golfer Ever?

108. *Tiger Woods: Son, Hero, and Champion.*
109. Quoted in Jaime Diaz, "Masters Plan," *Sports Illustrated*, April 13, 1998, p. 65.
110. Woods with Mitchell, *Playing Through*, p. 212.
111. Quoted in Strege, *Tiger*, p. 108.
112. Quoted in Strege, *Tiger*, p. 160.
113. Rosaforte, *Tiger Woods*, p. 173.
114. Quoted in Smith, "The Chosen One," p. 41.
115. John Feinstein, *The First Coming: Tiger Woods: Master or Martyr?* New York: Ballantine, 1998, p. 63.
116. Quoted in Barton, "Mark McCormack," p. 214.
117. Quoted in Steve Rushin, "Out of the Woods," *Sports Illustrated*, April 20, 1998, p. 36.
118. Doug Ferguson, "Woods Looking To Be 'Major' Contender Again," Associated Press, June 16, 1998.
119. Gary Van Sickle, "GolfPlus: Teeing Off," *Sports Illustrated*, July 27, 1998, p. G28.
120. Quoted in John Garrity, "Double Major," *Sports Illustrated*, July 27, 1998, p. 46.
121. Transcript of Tiger Woods interview with the media August 13 at the PGA Championship in Redmond, Washington. Available at www.pgatour.com.
122. Quoted in Stephen Wade, "O'Meara Tops Woods in Match

Play," Associated Press, October 18, 1998.

123. Quoted in "Quotable," *Milwaukee Journal-Sentinel,* October 20, 1998, sec. C, p. 1.

124. Quoted in Gordon Sakamoto, "Woods Beats Singh with Birdie," Associated Press, November 19, 1998.

125. Quoted in Kirkpatrick, "A Tiger in the Grass," p. 72.

126. Quoted in Rosaforte, *Tiger Woods,* p. 148.

127. Quoted in Jim Litke, "Tiger Woods Won't Win the PGA Championship," Associated Press, August 16, 1998.

128. Transcript of Tiger Woods interview with the media August 13 at the PGA Championship in Redmond, Washington.

129. Transcript of Tiger Woods interview with the media August 23 at the World Series of Golf PGA in Akron, Ohio. Available at www.pgatour.com.

130. Quoted in Jaime Diaz, "All Eyes on Tiger," *Sports Illustrated,* January 13, 1997, p. 7.

131. *Tiger Woods: Son, Hero, and Champion.*

132. Quoted in Smith, "The Chosen One," p. 44.

133. Quoted in White, "I'm Just Who I Am," p. 33.

Important Dates in the Life of Tiger Woods

December 30, 1975
Born Eldrick Thon Woods in Cypress, California, to Earl and Kultida Woods; nicknamed "Tiger" by his father.

October 6, 1978
At age two makes his first network television appearance on the *Mike Douglas Show* and putts against Bob Hope; he is also featured in this year in a story on a Los Angeles television station.

December 29, 1979
One day before his fourth birthday, shoots a round of 48 for nine holes at the Navy Destroyer Golf Course in Cypress.

1981
Appears on the network television show *That's Incredible.*

1982
By age six has already made two holes-in-one.

1984
Wins the Optimist International Junior World age bracket championship for golfers eight to ten; wins a record five more age bracket championships at the ages of nine, twelve, thirteen, fourteen, and fifteen.

1989
Finishes second in the prestigious Insurance Youth Golf Classic National.

1990
Becomes the youngest champion in the Insurance Youth Golf

Classic National; finishes second in the PGA National Junior Championship; goes to Paris, France, to compete in the Southern California–French Junior Cup; is a semifinalist at the U.S. Junior Amateur Championship; is named Southern California Player of the Year.

1991

Becomes the youngest to win the U.S. Junior Amateur Championship; wins sixth Optimist International Junior World title, the Southern California Junior Championship, the PING/Phoenix Junior, and the Orange Bowl Junior International; plays in the U.S. Amateur Championship; is named *Golf Digest* Player of the Year and Titleist-*Golfweek* National Amateur of the Year.

1992

Becomes the youngest person to play in a Professional Golfers Association (PGA) tour event, the Los Angeles Open; repeats as U.S. Junior Champion; wins the Insurance Youth Golf Classic; finishes in the top thirty-two of the U.S. Amateur Championship.

1993

Wins third U.S. Junior Championship and Southern California Junior Best Ball Championship; finishes in the top thirty-two of the U.S. Amateur Championship; plays in the PGA tour's Nissan Los Angeles Open, Honda Classic, GTE Byron Nelson Classic; named *Golf World* Player of the Year; wins Dial Award for top national high school athlete; accepts a scholarship to attend Stanford in 1994.

August 26, 1994

Becomes the youngest to win the U.S. Men's Amateur Championship. In 1994 graduates from Western High School; member of the U.S. squad that wins the U.S. World Amateur Team Championships in Versailles, France; wins the Western Amateur Team Championship; the William Tucker Invitational, his first college event; the Jerry Pate Invitational; plays in the professional Asian Classic in Thailand and the Nestle Invitational, Buick Classic, and Motorola Western Open PGA tour events; named *Golf World* Man of the Year.

1995
Repeats as U.S. Men's Amateur champion; wins Stanford Invitational; tied for forty-first at Masters, where he is the only amateur to make the cut, and plays in three professional tournaments including the U.S. Open; ties for fifth at the NCAA Championship; member of the U.S. Walker Cup team.

1996
On August 25 becomes the first to win three consecutive U.S. Men's Amateur Championships; as an amateur also wins the NCAA Championship; ties British Open amateur records for low total (281) and low round (66); is named Fred Haskins College Player of the Year and Jack Nicklaus College Player of the Year; August 29 makes his pro debut in the first round of the Greater Milwaukee Open; October 2–6 wins the Las Vegas Invitational for his first PGA tour victory; October 17–20, wins the Walt Disney World/Oldsmobile Classic; is voted PGA tour Rookie of the Year and *Sports Illustrated* Sportsman of the Year.

1997
January 9–12 wins the Mercedes Championship; in February wins the Asian Honda Classic in Thailand; April 10–13 wins the Masters, setting a dozen records with an 18-under total 270 for his first professional major; May 15–18 wins the GTE Byron Nelson Classic; July 3–6 wins the Motorola Western Open; sets PGA tour record with money winnings of $2.066 million in just sixteen events; is selected Associated Press Male Athlete of the Year and PGA Tour Player of the Year; earns the number-one ranking in the world.

1998
Wins the Johnnie Walker Classic in Thailand in February and the BellSouth Classic May 7–10; finishes third in British Open July 16-19; wins the Vardon Trophy for low scoring average on the PGA Tour at 69.1.

For Further Reading

William Durbin, *Tiger Woods*. Philadelphia: Chelsea House, 1998. A biography for younger readers that reports the basic facts about Woods's life through his debut as a professional golfer.

John Garrity, *Tiger Woods: The Making of a Champion*. New York: Simon & Schuster, 1997. Reprints of articles about Tiger Woods that have appeared through the years in *Sports Illustrated* magazine. Supplemented with original text by Garrity.

S. A. Kramer, *Tiger Woods: Golfing to Greatness*. New York: Random House, 1997. A simple but comprehensive biography about Tiger Woods. Recommended for the younger reader.

Jeff Savage, *Tiger Woods: King of the Course*. Minneapolis: Lerner, 1998. Aimed at younger readers, this book recounts Woods's amateur career, his debut as a professional, and his victory in the Masters.

Works Consulted

Books

John Feinstein, *The First Coming: Tiger Woods: Master or Martyr?* New York: Ballantine, 1998. In this short book, more an essay than a biography, the author dwells on just about every mistake he believes Earl and Tiger Woods have ever made. Despite his reputation as a fine sportswriter, Feinstein admits to a "feud" between himself and the Woodses over previous stories he has written; thus this book is written from an unfortunately biased perspective.

Bill Gutman, *Tiger Woods: A Biography.* New York. Pocket Book, 1997. A solid portrait of Tiger Woods by an author who has written many sports books, including a biography of Michael Jordan.

Tim Rosaforte, *Tiger Woods: The Makings of a Champion.* New York: St. Martin's Press, 1997. Rosaforte, who writes for *Sports Illustrated* magazine, documents how Woods grew up learning the game and carries the reader through Tiger's pro debut in 1996. This veteran sports writer displays a fine understanding of the game of golf as well as his subject.

Calvin H. Sinnette, *Forbidden Fairways: African Americans and the Game of Golf.* Chelsea, MI: Sleeping Bear Press, 1998. Sinnette showcases the struggles black golfers have gone through in their battle against racism, a fight that would one day allow Tiger Woods to become a superstar. His book is a definitive history of this subject.

John Strege, *Tiger: A Biography of Tiger Woods.* New York: Broadway Books, 1997. As a reporter for the *Orange County*

Register, Strege wrote many stories about Woods from age fourteen. This biography contains wonderful background information on how Woods developed his skills and grew up to be one of golf's greatest players.

Earl Woods with Fred Mitchell, *Playing Through: Straight Talk on Hard Work, Big Dreams, and Adventures with Tiger.* New York: HarperCollins, 1998. This second book by Earl Woods contains more biographical material on himself and his famous son than did his first book. Woods also uses the book to answer media criticism of himself on a variety of subjects.

Earl Woods with Pete McDaniel, *Training a Tiger: A Father's Guide to Raising a Winner in Both Golf and Life.* New York: HarperCollins, 1997. Earl Woods, in his first book, explains how he taught his son to play golf from toddlerhood. Although it contains some biographical information about Tiger, this book is designed to show parents how to develop relationships with their children while teaching them to play golf.

Periodicals

Jonathan Abrahams, "Golden Child or Spoiled Brat?" *Golf Magazine,* April 1998, pp. 56–65.

John Barton, "Mark McCormack," *Golf Digest,* June 1998, pp. 202–26.

Tom Callahan, "In Search of Tiger Phong," *Golf Digest,* October 1997, pp. 64–80.

Tom Callahan, "Is This Kid Superman?" *Golf Digest,* November 1996, pp. 56–63.

Tom Callahan, "The Epilogue: A Downpayment on a Dream," *Golf Digest,* November 1997, pp. 45–46.

Jaime Diaz, "All Eyes on Tiger," *Sports Illustrated,* January 13, 1997, pp. 4–7.

Jaime Diaz, "Masters Plan," *Sports Illustrated,* April 13, 1998, pp. 62–67.

John Garrity, "Double Major," *Sports Illustrated,* July 27, 1998, pp. 42–47.

Roy S. Johnson, "Tiger! The Sky's the Limit for Golf—the Game and the Business," *Fortune*, May 12, 1997, pp. 72–84.

Curry Kirkpatrick, "A Tiger in the Grass," *Newsweek*, April 10, 1995, pp. 70–72.

Curry Kirkpatrick, "Great Names, Great Games," *Newsweek*, December 26, 1994–January 2, 1995, pp. 114–15.

Hugh B. Price et al., "Black America and Tiger's Dilemma," *Ebony*, July 1997, pp. 28–34.

Rick Reilly, "For You Harvey," *Sports Illustrated*, April 17, 1995, pp. 16–23.

Rick Reilly, "Goodness Gracious, He's a Great Ball of Fire," *Sports Illustrated*, March 27, 1995, pp. 62–72.

Rick Reilly, "Strokes of Genius," *Sports Illustrated*, April 21, 1997, pp. 30–49.

Rick Reilly, "Top Cat," *Sports Illustrated*, October 28, 1996, pp. 46–50.

Chris Rice, "Why Tiger Makes Us Feel Good: Is the Best Remedy for Racism Visible Black Achievement?" *Christianity Today*, July 14, 1997, pp. 12–13.

Tim Rosaforte, "Follow the Leader," *Golf World*, July 11, 1997, pp. 18–24.

Tim Rosaforte, "The Comeback Kid," *Sports Illustrated*, September 5, 1994, pp. 14–16.

Jeff Rude, "Prince of Pebble, O'Meara Wins Despite Tiger on His Tail," *Golfweek*, February 8, 1997, pp. 1, 29.

Steve Rushin, "Out of the Woods," *Sports Illustrated*, April 20, 1998, pp. 32–37.

"Scorecard," *Sports Illustrated*, September 8, 1997, p. 21.

Eric L. Smith, "Eye of the Tiger," *Black Enterprise*, September 1997, pp. 90–91.

Gary Smith, "The Chosen One," *Sports Illustrated*, December 23, 1996, pp. 31–42.

Ron Stodghill II et al., "Tiger, Inc.," *Business Week*, April 28, 1997, pp. 32–36.

John Strege, "Tiger Woods Has Everyone's Attention. He's Talented, He's Exciting, He's Grrreat!" *Sports Illustrated for Kids*, August 1997, pp. 38–40.

Gary Van Sickle, "GolfPlus: Teeing Off," *Sports Illustrated*, July 27, 1998, p. G28.

Jack E. White, "I'm Just Who I Am," *Time*, May 5, 1997, pp. 32–36.

Isabel Wilkerson, "The All American," *Essence*, November 1997, pp. 99–104.

Newspapers

Gary D'Amato, "It's Official: Woods Era Dawns," *Milwaukee Journal-Sentinel*, August 29, 1996, pp. C1, C3.

Gary D'Amato and Dan Manoyan, "Woods Says His Pro Golf Debut Was Successful," *Milwaukee Journal-Sentinel*, September 3, 1996, p. C13.

Doug Ferguson, "Woods Looking To Be 'Major' Contender Again," Associated Press, June 16, 1998.

Jim Litke, "Tiger Woods Won't Win the PGA Championship," Associated Press, August 16, 1998.

"Quotable," *Milwaukee Journal-Sentinel*, October 20, 1998, sec. C, p. 1.

Stephen Wade, "O'Meara Tops Woods in Match Play," Associated Press, October 18, 1998.

Quoted in Gordon Sakamoto, "Woods Beats Singh with Birdie," Associated Press, November 19, 1998.

Videos

Highlights of the 1997 Masters Tournament. Warner Brothers. Monarch Home Video, 1997.

Tiger Woods: Son, Hero, and Champion. Trans World International. CBS Video, 1997.

Index

Picture Credits

About the Author

This is the sixth book written by Michael V. Uschan. His previous works include a biography of John F. Kennedy, *A Multicultural Portrait of World War I*, and *A Basic Guide to Luge*, part of a series written for the U.S. Olympic Committee. Mr. Uschan began his career as a writer and editor with United Press International, a wire service that provided news reports to newspapers, radio, and television. Because journalism is sometimes called "history in a hurry," he considers writing history books a natural extension of the skills he developed as a journalist. The author still writes about sports for Associated Press, on topics from golf to Olympic speedskating. He and his wife, Barbara, live in Franklin, Wisconsin, a suburb of Milwaukee.